NATION OR EMPIRE?
THE DEBATE OVER
AMERICAN FOREIGN POLICY

Studies in International Affairs Number 10

Studies in International Affairs Number 10

NATION OR EMPIRE? THE DEBATE OVER AMERICAN FOREIGN POLICY

by Robert W. Tucker

The Washington Center of Foreign Policy Research
School of Advanced International Studies
The Johns Hopkins University

The Johns Hopkins Press, Baltimore and London

The Johns Hopkins Press, Baltimore, Maryland 21218
The Johns Hopkins Press Ltd., London

Standard Book Number (clothbound edition) 8018-0638-0
Standard Book Number (paperback edition) 8018-0639-9

Originally published, 1968
Johns Hopkins Paperbacks edition, 1968
Second printing, 1969

FOREWORD

Americans—surely the most introspective people on earth—have continually examined, interpreted, questioned, and expounded the distinctive nature of their polity and its role in the world. Their introspection has eagerly fed upon internal crises and external wars—indeed, upon anything that has called into question America's vitality, power, or security.

Now the convergence of entanglement in the painful war in Vietnam with the rise of domestic unrest in the nation has generated another wave of self-examination. But it is not clear how deeply this self-examination will penetrate. From the quality of the public discussion of American policy so far, one might conclude that self-examination will probe no further than the particular characteristics of the war and the domestic crisis without coming to grips with fundamental issues of American interests, power, and role. That would be unfortunate, since current events raise issues that are as critical for the next two decades as they were pertinent to the last two.

Professor Tucker takes the present convergence of internal and external troubles and the controversy it has generated as the point of departure for reexamining the underlying premises of American policy—particularly the premises about American security. His essay, like Professor Liska's *War and Order: Reflections on Vietnam and History*, contributes a longer-range perspective and a more profound dimension of analysis to the current re-assessment of American policy.

ROBERT E. OSGOOD
Director
Washington Center of
Foreign Policy Research

CONTENTS

NATION OR EMPIRE?
THE DEBATE OVER
AMERICAN FOREIGN POLICY

Studies in International Affairs Number 10

I. THE SIGNIFICANCE OF THE DEBATE

That American foreign policy is a matter of debate today is, in itself, neither unusual nor startling. Throughout the nation's history, and particularly since the close of the nineteenth century, debate over foreign policy has been the norm rather than the exception. During the last thirty years we have had an almost continuous debate—or series of debates. There is no need to examine here the many reasons for the seemingly endemic controversies that attend the diplomacy of what one foreign observer has termed "the most verbose democracy in the world."[1] Suffice it to say that controversy over the substance and conduct of foreign policy is a well-established tradition; it is unlikely to disappear in the foreseeable future.

At the same time, it is true that the intensity of the recurring debates over American foreign policy has varied, and considerably so. On this basis alone the period since 1965 surely merits distinction. For whatever the lasting significance of the present debate there can be little doubt about the passions it has aroused. One must go back to the controversy over intervention in the years prior to 1941 to find a debate comparable in its intensity. The debate attending the Truman Doctrine and the initiation of the policy of containment, significant as it undoubtedly was, neither reached nor sustained a comparable intensity. This is also true of the contro-

[1] Raymond Aron, "Reflections on American Diplomacy," *Daedalus* (Fall 1962), p. 719.

versies from the late forties to the middle sixties, with the possible exception of Korea. And even Korea does not provide a close parallel to Vietnam, at least with respect to the scope, depth, and persistence of the dissatisfaction Vietnam has engendered.

The present debate is not only distinctive because of its intensity. It is also unusual in terms of its participants. Indeed, the intensity must in large measure be explained by the identity of the participants. The debate has not followed party lines and it could scarcely have aroused the passions it has on the basis of party. It is doubtful, moreover, whether the established party structure any longer affords a basis for serious conflict over foreign policy. It last did so in the years before and during World War II as a result of a growing separation between liberalism and isolationism and the almost exclusive identification of the latter with conservative Republicanism. Korea again appears to be an exception. Yet in 1952 when public confusion and frustration reached proportions that could be effectively exploited by the party in opposition, the exploitation did not consist in rejecting the general policy that had led to the Korean intervention. And once in power the new Republican administration was quite faithful in continuing and building upon the Asian containment policy initiated by its predecessor. What the Korean and more recent examples demonstrate is simply that in the competition of parties for power, it remains an accepted rule of the game for opponents to capitalize on each other's difficulties and errors, despite the previous support of policies that led to these difficulties and errors. Opportunism is readily tolerated, if not a canon of the political game. But to the extent that recent debates over foreign policy have followed party lines, and have been motivated by normal considerations of political advantage, they have been neither profound nor bitter. It is difficult to see them becoming so.

What has given the present debate much of its intensity is the fact that the principal participants are former allies who had long been committed to the same causes. It is the mutual sense of betrayal that has done what normal party politics no longer seem able to do. For the most articulate and effective criticism of the Johnson administration and its supporters has come from the ranks of those who have provided the main support for American foreign policy since World War II, the liberal intellectuals and the moderate Republicans. The emergence of the "new left" and of an amorphous peace movement has no doubt, contributed considerably to the controversy. But these groups have been comprised for the most part of individuals who have never had a strong sense of identity with American foreign policy. This is clearly the case with the new left and allied groups for whom the war in Vietnam has provided an opportunity—a golden opportunity to be sure—they probably would have sought in any event. It is less true of the peace movement, or of that part of the peace movement distinct from the new left, which comprises many whose interest has been limited to the war in Vietnam and who have no apparent desire to confront the establishment on other issues, domestic or foreign. Indeed, many in the peace movement are political moderates on domestic issues and have given varying degrees of support to American foreign policy in the past. At any rate, whatever the long-run influence on foreign policy of a growing radicalization of American politics, its present impact is easily exaggerated. It is not the opposition of those who have never really formed a part of the foreign policy consensus that is the significant feature of the present debate, but the substantial defection of those who have formed a critical part of this consensus for the past generation.

How are we to account for this defection and particularly for the substantial defection and disaffection of the intellectuals? One of the more striking attempts to explain the intellectuals' defection has recently been made by Irving Kristol, who sees in it the dead, though still constraining, hand of the past and the harbinger of ominous ambitions for the future. A small minority apart, the American intellectual, Kristol writes, "is committed in the most profound way to a whole set of assumptions and ideas that are rooted in the 'isolationist' era of American history, and he cannot depart from these assumptions and ideas without a terrible sense of self-betrayal."[2] It is not only that the intellectual class cannot make the necessary adjustment to America's new imperial role in the world but that it would not do so even if it could. And it would not do so because "this crisis of the intellectual class in the face of an imperial destiny coincides with an internal power struggle within the United States itself. Our intellectuals are moving toward a significant 'confrontation' with the American 'establishment' and will do nothing to strengthen the position of their antagonist. Which is to say that the American intellectual class actually has an interest in thwarting the evolution of any kind of responsible and coherent

[2] Irving Kristol, "American Intellectuals and Foreign Policy," *Foreign Affairs* (July 1967), p. 605.

imperial policy."[3] This interest—nourished by a sense of grievance and resentment toward a society that refuses to accord intellectuals their just deserts —will presumably find its political expression in a "mass party of the ideological left," the basis of which will be the campus rather than the factory. In the campus groups protesting the war in Vietnam we may already see the beginnings of a serious movement into politics proper.

The principal difficulty with Kristol's argument is not in his refusal to take the present debate seriously by dealing with the intellectuals' opposition in terms of its intrinsic strengths and weaknesses. (It is even understandable that he refuses to do so. After all, those who reject the "imperatives of imperial power" and resist what history has decreed scarcely deserve to have their arguments taken seriously. One can only ask what has made them what they are and, if they are at all rational, what purposes their arguments are intended to serve.) It is simply that Kristol has drawn a picture of the American intellectual in his relation to foreign policy which is at considerable variance with reality. In doing so, the significance of the present dissatisfaction with American foreign policy is in large measure obscured, if not misrepresented. It is not true that apart from a very small minority the "American intellectual class" is solidly arrayed against the nation's foreign policy. It is not even true that, a very small minority apart, the intellectuals have been united in their opposition to the war in Vietnam. (There is, as should be apparent, a difference between the two, even if it is assumed that the war in Vietnam is but the

[3] *Ibid.*, p. 606.

prime manifestation of what is generally an imperial policy.) On the contrary, until the winter of 1967–68 a substantial percentage of the academic community either favored or were not markedly opposed to or were simply indifferent toward administration policy in Vietnam. That this percentage was considerably smaller than the corresponding percentage of the general public does not make it insignificant.

More important, however, if we consider the character of the intellectual opposition, which developed in the course of the war, we find that it has comprised at least three quite disparate groups. There have been those who have rather faithfully supported American foreign policy for a generation and then found themselves opposed to the war in Vietnam, though certainly not to the whole of American foreign policy. This group is by no means pacifist in commitment and has not ostensibly opposed the war on moral grounds, though it has not been insensitive to the moral issues raised by the war. (Many among this group endorsed American aims in Vietnam, supported at least some involvement in the conflict, and began to oppose the administration only after the war, and American involvement in the war, went beyond the pre-1965 level.) There are those who have formed a part of the peace movement, who are in varying degree pacifist in commitment and who have opposed the war chiefly on moral grounds. This second group has consisted of many who have not been hostile to American foreign policy in the past, at least when it did not involve the use of force. Finally, there are those who have condemned not only the war in Vietnam but the whole of American foreign policy and who have coupled this condemnation of foreign policy with an equally sweeping condemnation of domestic policy. The former has been found to grow out of, and to reflect, the latter. Both have been seen to need thoroughgoing reform, if not revolution.

There are no reliable studies that show how these three groups have compared in relative strength. But there is no persuasive reason for assuming that the third group has been numerically or otherwise stronger than the first two groups. If anything, the more reasonable assumption is that it has been the smallest of the three. Of the first two groups, there is not the slightest evidence to support the contention that they have desired a "significant confrontation with the American establishment." Quite the contrary, many of the first group, when not actually forming a part of the establishment, have been accused of being far too compliant. Whatever the merit of this accusation, it is ludicrous to see in this group a serious challenge to the status quo, whether at home or abroad. The peace groups, by and large, sprang up in response to the expanding American commitment in Vietnam and are likely to disappear with the war. They do not constitute a cohesive political group, and they have very little to say that is distinctive about American foreign policy beyond Vietnam, save that the nation must stay out of similar—or all—military involvements. Except for that part of the peace movement tied to the new left, they are relatively uninterested in domestic issues.

It is another matter entirely to find that the majority of American intellectuals continue to betray in varying degree the residue of an isolationist past. It would be astonishing were this not the case. It is not apparent, however, that this characteristic sets them apart from the rest of society. Nor is it apparent that this characteristic has prevented most of them from accepting the new role that America has played since World War II. The support they have given American foreign policy over the past generation has been marked by misgivings and more than occasional criticism. But this, too, is scarcely cause for surprise. What is surprising is that they have given so little trouble until very recently. Thus it is only in very recent years that opposition to the primacy of foreign over domestic policy has taken an active political form rather than a merely literary expression and this despite the undoubted domestic orientation of most American intellectuals (again, an orientation they share with the general public). There are reasons, discussed below, which partly explain this passivity before the reversal of a tradition as deeply rooted as any in American public life. The fact remains that until the Vietnamese war there was no widespread and insistent demand that the government abandon, or even seriously curtail, any of its major security policies in order to give greater attention, let alone a clear priority, to domestic needs. If that demand is insistent and widespread today it may or may not reflect a lingering commitment to, or recrudescence of, the isolationist ideal. The position that it must do so stems from the dogma that the American commitment in Vietnam throughout its successive phases has been the inescapable response to America's objective security needs and to her unavoidable responsibilities as a world power. This dogma forms the vital nerve of indictments like Irving Kristol's of the intellectuals' opposition to foreign policy. If it is accepted, the choice that must be made—if we may still call it a choice—is between acknowledging the imperatives of imperial power, as these imperatives have been broadly defined by the present administration, and railing against these imperatives out of a desire somehow to return to an isolationist past. If it is not accepted, it clearly does not follow that one must be an isolationist to protest against an imperial destiny for America, particularly an imperial destiny that results in the kind of war we have waged in Vietnam. (Indeed, there are many who have accepted an imperial destiny for America—and an imperial rationale for intervention—yet opposed the war in Vietnam in terms of the specific circumstances attending this conflict.) But whether one accepts it or not the point remains that the intellectuals' commitment to an "American way of life," an ideal that is admittedly in some measure inseparable from America's isolationist past, does not distinguish him today from the general society of which he is a part.

We return to the question raised earlier: How are we to account for the debate over American foreign policy? What is the significance of the increasing dissent and opposition, particularly on the part of many who have long provided critical support for American foreign policy? The answer cannot be in doubt. It is the war in Vietnam that has given rise to most of the disaffection. It is the war in Vietnam that must explain, above all other considerations, the substantial defection and growing disaffection of the intellectuals. The best evidence for this is the relative absence of dissatisfaction with American foreign policy in the period immediately prior to the expansion of the war in the winter of 1965. A review of the period from the

Cuban missile crisis to the beginning of the aerial bombardment of North Vietnam leads to the conclusion, a striking conclusion in view of what has followed, that in terms of domestic dissent over foreign policy it has been one of the more tranquil in recent history. Yet with one exception American foreign policy was then substantially what it is now. And that one exception was already in a far more than embryonic stage. American commitments and policies have not changed. What has happened is that one of our promissory Asian notes has had to be met. If American foreign policy is interventionist now, it was also interventionist then. The American outlook and style remain the same now as they were then. None of this led to notable unrest or dissatisfaction. It is the war as such, the war taken in isolation from all other considerations, that has provided the principal and immediate cause of the debate. Vietnam clearly raises issues whose significance go well beyond the war. Even so, the debate would not have arisen, and probably could not have arisen, in the absence of the war we have waged in Vietnam.

It is also true that the debate would not have aroused the passions it has were it not for those features which set this war apart from other wars the nation has fought. Although some observers have sought to explain the intensity of dissent over Vietnam in terms of a changed attitude toward war,[4]

---

[4] Thus Richard Rovere has written: "Those who support the war, like those who oppose it, appeal not to the patriotic heart but to the bleeding one. This is without precedent." And he concludes that "there is building up in this country a powerful sentiment not simply against the war in Vietnam but against war itself, not simply against bombing in Viet-

it seems more plausible to explain the dissent in terms of the features that have marked this particular war. It is by now banal to say that from the very outset the war has seemed confusing, frustrating, and repugnant. Yet it has been all of these things. It has been a confusing war not only in its immediate origins but even in the identity of the adversary. It has been a frustrating war in the elusiveness, if not indefinability, of the objectives for which the war has ostensibly been fought and in the indifference, if not the unreliability, of those we have presumably sought to help. It has been a repugnant war not so much for the reason that it has claimed a larger portion of the noncombatant population than previous wars—indeed, we do not know that it has done so—but because the very nature of the war has not permitted a meaningful distinction between combatants and civilians. It has even been a humiliating war, given the disparity in power of the adversaries. The disparity could be glossed over for a time and pride assuaged if only by the device of making North Vietnam the proxy of China. But this device for creating a bigger and more worthy adversary is no longer persuasive. We have been, in fact, at war with a very small state, however much it has been supplied by its major allies, and the only thing more humiliating than being at war with so small a power is to be militarily frustrated, let alone defeated, by it.

---

nam but against bombing anywhere at any time for any reason, not simply against the slaughter of innocents in an unjust conflict but also against the slaughter of those who may be far from innocent in a just conflict." "Reflections: Half Out of Our Tree," *The New Yorker* (October 1967), p. 78.

In all these respects, as critics never tire of pointing out, Vietnam must be distinguished from our previous wars, and particularly the Korean War. Although the contrast with Korea is frequently overdrawn, it still has enough truth to be effective. In its immediate origins Korea did not raise the doubt and uncertainty, and even the suspicion of duplicity, that Vietnam has raised. If both Korea and Vietnam have been civil wars, which they have been, then we must still say that there are civil wars and civil wars and that the difference between them may be enormous. In Korea the initial objective of the war, to repel the aggressor, was neither elusive nor unobtainable. It was the subsequent and expanded objective of uniting Korea by force that provoked Chinese intervention and was considered, rightly or wrongly, unobtainable without running too great a risk of general war. Even so, the initial objective of the war was realized, and in all likelihood could have been realized much sooner had it not been made to depend on the disputed issue of prisoner-of-war repatriation.

There is no parallel here with Vietnam, just as there is no parallel in the morale and effectiveness of those on whose behalf we intervened in the two instances. Whereas the army of South Korea was an effective fighting force within six months of the outbreak of war, the army of South Vietnam has remained ineffective and unreliable despite years of American effort. In South Korea it was at least possible to distinguish between civilian and enemy combatant, given the absence of a guerrilla movement in the South and the hostility of the South Koreans to their invading northern brothers. In South Vietnam the difficulty of making this distinction cannot but prove morally debilitating, not only because of the actual quantity of death and destruction visited upon the civilian population but because of the circumstances in which this death and destruction occur. If killing the innocent is an evil whatever the circumstances, there is still a difference between doing so in a war that is broadly supported by the civilian population which must suffer the incidental if unavoidable consequences of military operations and doing so in a war that is, at best, borne indifferently by the affected population. This difference is all the more significant where the justification of military intervention is made to depend in large measure on the purpose of enabling a people freely to determine their destiny. Given this purpose, the will of a people to determine their destiny and to preserve their independence justifies, at least in part, the suffering inflicted on those who have taken no direct part in the war. In South Korea there was never much doubt about the quality of this will. In South Vietnam there has never been anything but doubt about it.

The latter considerations point to one side of the dilemma that has marked the administration's persistent attempts to provide a satisfactory rationale for the war in Vietnam. In the main, that rationale has followed two principal lines, at times emphasizing the one in preference to the other, more often combining the two with near equal emphasis. On the one hand, the American intervention has been justified in terms of the freedom and self-determination of the South Vietnamese. "Our objective," President Johnson declared in his first major address following the initiation of aerial bombardment against North Vietnam, "is the independence of

South Vietnam, and its freedom from attack. We want nothing for ourselves, only that the people of South Vietnam be allowed to guide their own country in their own way." On the other hand, the American intervention has been justified in terms of America's security interests, whether identified with the integrity and continued independence of the nations of Southeast Asia or with the containment of China throughout Asia or, more generally still, with the defense of world order. If in the later stages of the conflict the emphasis appeared to shift to America's security interests, they were never really absent from the administration's rationale for the war. Thus in the address cited above, the President, far from ignoring the nation's security interests, stated: "We fight because we must fight if we are to live in a world where every country can shape its own destiny. And only in such a world will our own freedom be finally secure." And further: "We are also there to strengthen world order. . . . To leave Vietnam to its fate would shake the confidence . . . in the value of American commitment, the value of America's word. The result would be increased unrest and instability, and even wider war." Three weary and frustrating years later, in his dramatic announcement that he would neither seek nor accept another term in office, the President declared: ". . . the heart of our involvement in South Vietnam has always been America's security. And the larger purpose of our involvement has always been to help the nations of Southeast Asia become independent, self-sustaining members of the world community, at peace with themselves and with all others." The same theme has been echoed on countless occasions by administration spokesmen. We are in South Viet-

nam not only for the South Vietnamese but for ourselves, not only to preserve the freedom of the
South Vietnamese but to preserve the freedom of
others and ultimately, of our own. What we are doing directly for the South Vietnamese (and indirectly
for others) we are also doing for ourselves, and
what we fail to do for others we fail to do for
ourselves. The attempt to distinguish between the
disinterested and the interested elements in the
American rationale for the war thus appears almost
superfluous, and even misleading.

There is nothing novel in this theme, particularly
in the fusion of the interested and disinterested elements which together comprise the American rationale for the war. Essentially the same theme, with
the same fusion of arguments, formed the rationale
of the policy of containment when it was initiated
in 1947. In what is now the historic expression of
that policy, the Truman Doctrine, President Truman
declared that a willingness "to help free people to
maintain their free institutions and their national
integrity against aggressive movements that seek
to impose upon them totalitarian regimes . . . is no
more than a frank recognition that totalitarian regimes imposed on free peoples, by direct or indirect
aggression, undermine the foundations of international peace and hence the security of the United
States." The assistance to Greece and Turkey, which
formed the immediate purpose of President Truman's address, was to be understood in these terms
as was the effort to reconstruct and defend western
Europe. The American intervention in the Korean
conflict followed along similar lines, as did the subsequent expansion of American commitments in Asia.
In 1960 a high official of the Johnson administra-

tion, in reflecting on the manner in which successive American administrations since the turn of the century have conceived of the nation's interests, summarized it in approving terms that might just as well have been written today for Vietnam: "It appears to be a characteristic of American history that this nation cannot be effective in its military and foreign policy unless it believes that both its security interests and its commitment to certain moral principles require the nation to act."[5]

What is novel, then, is clearly not the essential rationale that has been given for the war. Instead, it is the notable lack of success the administration has enjoyed in making this rationale persuasive, at least in making it persuasive to many who have afforded support in the recent past for American foreign policy. The justification of the American intervention in terms of defending the freedom and self-determination of the South Vietnamese people could prove persuasive only to the degree that the people defended manifested a will for freedom and self-determination. Doubt over the quality of this will placed in doubt the justification, and surely the wisdom, for intervening: it also gave rise to fears that the intervention could ultimately succeed only by perverting the very principle on behalf of which war was undertaken. For in the absence of sufficient will on the part of those to be defended, they could be successfully defended only by creating a highly dependent relationship between the defended and their defenders. The danger that this would prove to be the outcome in South Vietnam, that America's intervention would prove as debilitating

[5] W. W. Rostow, *The United States in the World Arena* (1960), p. 547.

to the defenders as to the defended, was apparent from the start and grew as the war progressed. It not only raised the question whether intervention could be successfully undertaken in the circumstances that characterized South Vietnam, but whether, given these circumstances, intervention ought ever to be undertaken in the absence of other, and compelling, interests.

To be sure, if other compelling interests can be shown to be in jeopardy as a result of a failure to intervene, there is no need to justify intervention in terms of the good conferred upon the defended. Nor is it necessary that these other, and compelling, interests comprise only a concern of the intervening state for its own security. But despite a generation of "world leadership," and the steady habituation of the public to the real or alleged necessities arising therefrom, it is still essential for an American government, if it is to provide a persuasive justification for intervention, to show that the failure to intervene in a given instance will have markedly adverse consequences for the nation's security. The dilemma of the Johnson administration has been its apparent inability successfully to represent the war in Vietnam either as a vindication of the principles of freedom and self-determination or as a measure indispensable for American security. Whether such representation could have been successfully made at all, whether the nature of the case permitted it to be made, is not in question here, but only the failure the administration has experienced in presenting a persuasive rationale for the war.

It will not do to explain this failure simply in terms of the intrinsic, and perhaps even the unique, difficulties that have arisen in the course of the

Vietnamese war. Nor will it suffice to account for the significance of the present debate simply in terms of these difficulties. Although the debate would not have occurred in the absence of the war, and although the intensity of passion thereby aroused would not have been as great if the war had been fought in less difficult circumstances it does not follow that the significance of the debate must be found merely in the fact that we have engaged in a particularly distasteful and difficult war. The meaning of Vietnam, and the significance of the debate it has engendered, is not, as some have insisted, simply that we chose a very poor place to wage a war, whatever the reasons for doing so, though this we surely did. It is not simply a gigantic piece of bad luck, though this it surely is. If the present debate would not have arisen in the absence of the war, if the passions aroused would not have been as great in a war fought in less difficult circumstances, the question persists why we chose to intervene in circumstances so unpromising. Is the significance of Vietnam that it has revealed, and revealed in the most dramatic manner, the inadequacies of the methods by which the nation conducts its foreign policy, inadequacies that reflect not only upon the bureaucracy charged with the conduct of foreign policy but upon the nature of the relations between bureaucracy and public? Is the significance of Vietnam that it has revealed the shortcomings of a philosophy of incrementalism when it is taken from its appropriate democratic domestic setting and applied to the far less favorable environment of state relations? Is the significance of Vietnam that it has revealed what can happen as a result of "a long exercise in national inadvertance, of a long series of partial decisions, none of them taken with any clear comprehension of the depths of involvement to which they were bringing us"?[6]

No doubt, this view, which finds in Vietnam a striking failure of the entire foreign policy mechanism, is a signal part of the truth. Yet it is difficult to believe that it is the whole truth or even that it is the most important truth about Vietnam. If it were, Vietnam must be seen as an unfortunate application of an otherwise sound and desirable policy, to be accounted for in terms of bad luck and inadequate method. The significance of the debate, apart from its purely domestic overtones, would then be reduced to a debate over method (it is hardly possible to do a great deal about bad luck). This view may be and is shared in varying degree by many critics, whose differences with the administration are of less magnitude than they frequently believe. It is not shared, however, by the administration and its supporters. If the latter are all too willing to admit to bad luck, if they are prepared even to acknowledge in moments of candor some inadequacy of method, they have consistently refused to see in Vietnam the misapplication of an otherwise sound and desirable policy. There is no apparent reason why they should not be taken at their word. Nor is it apparent that they are wrong in contending that the intervention in Vietnam was no misapplication of an otherwise sound policy but one possible outcome which has always been implicit in this policy.

[6] George F. Kennan, "The Quest for Concept in American Foreign Policy," *Harvard Today* (September 1967), p. 16.

If Vietnam has a significance that goes beyond the issue of method, if it has an importance that transcends the war itself, it must be seen in the policy—and outlook—that made Vietnam an ever-present possibility. That policy and outlook are not simply the work of the Johnson administration, as some critics would have us believe, just as they are not the work of its immediate predecessor. The essential elements of America's present Asian policy were determined in the course of the war in Korea. In fashioning these elements of policy, the Truman administration applied to Asia a more general policy it had already applied to Europe, a general policy that since its first expression in March 1947 had become known as the Truman Doctrine. In doing so, the Truman administration was not blind to the obvious differences between Europe and Asia. Nor have succeeding administrations been blind to these differences. Then as now, however, an awareness of the huge disparities between Europe and Asia has not dissuaded four successive administrations from attempting to contain communist power in Asia, whether Soviet, North Korean, Chinese, or North Vietnamese, and to do so, as we have already observed, in terms of the same rationale, the same fusion of interested and altruistic reason, given today for the war in Vietnam. Then as now American power and leadership were to be employed to create and maintain a stable world order, an order which would enable peoples to work out their own destinies in their own way and, by enabling them to do so, thereby insure American security. If the present debate over American foreign policy has a significance that transcends Vietnam it is because it again raises the issues of the Truman Doctrine, issues that concern the scope, ideological temper, means, and purposes of American foreign policy. But it does so in circumstances substantially different from the circumstances of a generation ago. Therein must be found the broader significance of the debate, for the changes that have occurred require us to look at issues that have persisted for a generation in a new light and to invest them with new meaning.

It is not the novelty, then, of the arguments marking the present debate that ultimately must give it a significance greater than Vietnam, but the novelty of the environment in which the arguments are made. Indeed, what is striking in the present debate is the remarkable continuity of the arguments with those of a generation ago. This is evidently true of the official rationale given for American foreign policy. There are some variations in theme; it would be astonishing if there were not, given the changes that have occurred in intervening years. Thus the goal of encouraging the growth of autonomous, if interdependent, regional security systems, while by no means new, has been given greater emphasis than in the past. Whatever its merits and prospects, this emphasis on regionalism is at once the acknowledgment of a growing insistence upon autonomy and the disavowal of a desire to build an empire of satellites. It represents the American middle ground between nationalism and universalism, the one deemed undesirable and the other considered—reluctantly—unattainable, and it permits—if only in aspiration—the devolution of responsibility. So, too, the shift in emphasis from containment to world order reflects both the relative success of the policy of containment and the expansion concomitant with that success of American interests and the diversity of possible threats to them. If these shifts in emphasis are not without importance, they nevertheless have left unaltered the essential rationale for American policy.

The same must be said for the criticism presently made of American foreign policy. Thus what is criticized as "globalism" today was also criticized in an earlier period. Globalism is a sin that has many meanings, but none of these meanings was unknown to the critics of a generation ago (some of whom are still the critics of today). The perfect expression of it is, of course, the Truman Doctrine, with its apparently unlimited and consequently indiscriminate commitment—"We must assist free peoples to work out their destinies in their own way"—its sense of universal crisis—"At the present moment in world history every nation must choose between alternative ways of life"—and its messianic hope of redeeming history—"To insure the peaceful development of nations, free from coercion . . . to make possible lasting freedom and independence for all. . . ." The prospect of an overextended America, committed by an indiscriminate anticommunism to intervene anywhere and everywhere in order to maintain the status quo, was raised then as it is raised still more insistently today. And although the great transformation of American foreign policy did not coincide with a domestic crisis, then as now critics predicted that globalism must eventually erode American political institutions and subvert domestic efforts at reform.

If this criticism has an impact today that it did not have before, if it enjoys a degree of acceptance that it did not enjoy a generation ago, the reasons must be found in the circumstances in which it is made. It is not simply that the rhetoric of yesterday has increasingly become the reality of today, that the Truman Doctrine has become policy whereas before it was little more than aspiration. It is that the rhetoric of yesterday has increasingly become the reality of today in circumstances that bear only a limited resemblance to the circumstances of yesterday. Whatever the declared scope and aspiration of the Truman Doctrine, the policy of containment to which it gave rise, as indeed the Doctrine itself, was primarily a response to what was considered at the time a serious and direct threat to American security resulting from the postwar weakness and instability of western Europe. The initial measures of containment, the Marshall Plan and the North Atlantic Alliance, formally expressed, and thereby made unmistakable, the vital American interest in preserving the security and independence of the nations of western Europe. In the context of Soviet-American rivalry, they constituted a clear acknowledgment that the domination of western Europe by the Soviet Union might shift the world balance of power decisively against the United States and thus open the Western Hemisphere to the encroachment of the adversary. At the very least, it was assumed that domination of Western Europe by the Soviet Union would result in a security problem for the United States the solution of which would severely strain the nation's resources and jeopardize its democratic institutions.

One may ask whether these assumptions were well-founded, whether by the late nineteen-forties the security of the United States was in fact so dependent on the maintenance of a balance of power in Europe. In retrospect, a case can be made that this dependence was exaggerated, that the structure and bases of power had already changed in ways which made the security of America much less dependent upon a European balance of power than only a decade before, and that the prospect had already arisen of a security—at least, a physical security—no longer dependent on what transpired outside the Western Hemisphere. It is not surprising, however, that a persuasive case to this effect was not made at the time. If security policies point to the future, as they necessarily must do, the standards they erect are largely anchored in the past. It is men's experience rather than, or more than, their reason that is the decisive influence in the judgments they make on their security. In the case of America in the late forties the most relevant experience was, of course, the period preceding and including World War II, an experience that seemed to demonstrate conclusively the intimate dependence of American security on a European balance of power. To be sure, this immediate experience has to be placed against the background of the more general experience of isolationism, that is, the period of well over a century when American security appeared as unconditioned by events outside the hemisphere. But it was precisely this more general experience of free, and seemingly unconditioned, security that accentuated the sense of insecurity when it did finally occur. In view of the nation's experience from the early nineteenth century to the nineteen-thirties, the period that followed and that culminated in the early years of the cold war was bound to provoke a strong, in retrospect perhaps an exaggerated, sense of insecurity.

These considerations may be seen to qualify the nature and magnitude of the security problem that confronted the nation in the late forties. They hardly established the proposition that America did not face a serious security problem in this period. If the threat to a nation's security admittedly depends upon a judgment that is ultimately subjective, it does not follow that all judgments respecting security are somehow equal, or, as some would have it, are equally suspect. Nations are more secure or less secure. There are objective criteria by which their degree of security or insecurity may be determined. How insecure America would have been had the nations of western Europe fallen under communist control may be disputed. That America would have been much less secure hardly seems open to doubt.

This emphasis on the security motive in the early policy of containment need not, and should not, be pushed to the point of excluding other considerations. Containment in Europe was not undertaken solely for reasons of security, narrowly construed, and no one contended so at the time. Considerations of political and cultural affinity were evidently very important. Moreover, the security motive itself was not clearly separated from other, and broader, considerations, as, indeed, it has seldom been so separated in American diplomacy. The security of America was not seen as something apart from the broader purpose of America abroad. Then as now the preservation of values and institutions identified with the life of the nation was seen to require an external environment whose characteristics extended beyond the requirements of a balance of power. Then as now the conviction persisted that the preservation of the institutions of freedom in America is dependent upon their preservation—or eventual realization—elsewhere in the world. Then as now security was interpreted as a function both of a balance of power between states and of the internal order maintained by states. Finally, then as now the concern for order—identified, in principle, with the proscription of force between states—formed a general, yet important, element of policy.

But if it is true that the security motive in the early policy of containment included a broader motive for policy as well, if it is true that American security and the American purpose of preserving and extending freedom were never clearly separated, it is still the case that a narrower and more traditional conception of security—security interpreted as a function of a balance of power—received the greater emphasis. One may say that if containment always implied a concept of world order, which it evidently did, there was still a difference between the two, if only as a matter of emphasis and priority. Whatever the larger implications of the Truman Doctrine, the policy of containment as initially applied to Europe was more or less synonymous with a balance-of-power policy. The security interest of containment overrode all other considerations. And it was the primacy of the security interest, which found its principal expression in America's European policy, that largely neutralized the criticism made against the larger implications of American policy.

These same considerations help to explain the relative absence of dissent to the intervention in Korea as well as to other measures taken in Asia concomitantly with that intervention, measures which laid the basis of American containment policy in Asia. It is ironic that the decision which, more than any other decision, determined America's postwar Asian policy provoked so little controversy at the time it was taken. In some measure, the explanation is to be found in the events immediately marking the outbreak of the Korean conflict and particularly the fortuitous circumstances which permitted the United Nations Security Council to sanction the American action in Korea. Far more significant, however, was the apparent threat to Japanese security held out by the aggression against South Korea, if that aggression were to go unopposed. But the most important consideration, the consideration that seems to have overshadowed all others, was simply the connection drawn, whether rightly or wrongly, between Korea and western Europe. The attack upon South Korea in June 1950 followed closely upon the coup in Czechoslovakia, the blockade of Berlin, the first Soviet explosion of an atomic device and the Chinese communist accession to power. These events were widely interpreted as a mounting communist offensive which was increasingly taking a military form and which, if left unopposed, might well eventuate in an armed attack against western Europe. During the first year of the Korean War, and even after, the fear that Europe might be attacked was deep and persistent. It was this fear that above all else explains the relative absence of dissent to the Korean intervention and, indeed, to the other measures taken in Asia at the same time. And it was the primacy of the security interest at the time of Korea, an interest centered in Europe, that largely neutralized early criticism of extending American containment policy to Asia.

In the decade following the initiation of containment, Korea stands out as the decisive event in the evolution of American policy. The Korean experience largely determined the form and course that the great transformation in American foreign policy eventually took. At the outbreak of the Korean War, it was uncertain whether America would extend its alliance commitments beyond the Western Hemisphere, the North Atlantic region, and the defensive perimeter in the Pacific running from the Ryukyus to the Philippine Islands. Even within the area of commitment, the means by which America would implement its commitment to western Europe remained uncertain. Korea put an end to these uncertainties. In Europe, the Korean conflict led to the re-establishment of American forces, the establishment of an integrated command structure, the decision to rearm Germany, and the agreement on a common defense strategy. In Asia, the Korean War led to American intervention in the Chinese civil conflict and prompted the conclusion of a series of bilateral and multilateral alliances that continue today roughly to define the extent of the American commitment in that area.

The wisdom of this sudden extension of containment to Asia, where it was to apply primarily as a barrier to Chinese expansion, did not pass unchallenged. To most critics it appeared, and continues to appear today, as the misapplication of a strategy that was sound only when applied to Europe. (To a few critics the predominantly military form eventually assumed by containment was misguided even as applied to Europe, let alone as applied to Asia.) In brief the criticism went as follows: Whereas in Europe military containment was undertaken primarily in response to the threat of an overt armed attack, and on behalf of nations only temporarily weak, in Asia military containment would have to be undertaken in response to threats that primarily took the form of civil conflicts, though aided in varying degree from outside, and on behalf of nations that were likely to remain weak and divided for a very long time. Whereas in Europe American alliance policy was directed against a conventional military threat, in Asia it was directed against a threat that fed upon and exploited—though it did not create—genuinely revolutionary conditions. Whereas in Europe American policy had the support of those we sought to protect, in Asia this support was lacking on the whole. Thus even when Chinese expansion assumed a predominantly military character, it would do so in ways (subversion, indirect aggression) which normally could not be countered by a strategy that had been effective in Europe. With few exceptions, alliances with Asian states had no solid foundation, did not express a mutuality of benefits and liabilities, and did not respond to American interests in the area, which are primarily political rather than military. Moreover, given the obvious differences between Europe and Asia, the attempt to carry out a policy of military containment in Asia could not avoid the likelihood of creating highly dependent—that is, imperial—relationships. Finally, in this earlier period as today, it was argued that even where the effort to contain communist expansion through military means might prove relatively effective, it must result in the overextension of American power.

At the root of this criticism over American containment policy in Asia, and more particularly of the means by which this policy was to be implemented, is a persistent and substantial, though frequently obscured, disagreement over the nature of American interests in Asia and, indeed, in the world at large. That disagreement, it is true, cannot be usefully considered without regard to the quantity and quality of American power as well as the circumstances in which this power must be employed. To the extent, however, that criticism of American containment policy in Asia is made to turn on the question of American capabilities, it obscures the vital issue of the interests that policy is presumably intended to serve, quite apart from the power available for realizing these interests. Yet the issue of interests is critical if for no other reason than that the insistence on the limits of American power has been as misleading as it has been well-founded. In an earlier period, as today, America's Asian policy has not so much exposed the limits of American power—at least, it has not done so in a literal sense—as it has raised the issue of the wisdom and desirability of the interests on behalf of which power is to be employed.[7] No doubt, interests are themselves determined by the price they entail, or the price they are expected to entail. But this truism only serves to emphasize, and particularly in America's case, the central importance of the issue of interests. In this sense, Vietnam is only the latest illustration of a continuing disagreement over the

[7] By "literal sense" I mean simply the material power of America and the limits of this power. Of course, our Asian policy has placed in question the willingness to employ this power beyond a certain point. But that willingness—or lack thereof—is itself inseparable from the issue of the wisdom and desirability of interests on behalf of which power is to be employed.

nature of American interests in Asia that is partly obscured by concentration on the limits of American power. Essentially what is at issue is a broad disparity of view over both the conditions, and even the very meaning, of American security and the other interests whose vindication would justify, if necessary, the use of American military power.

If this essential issue was not clearly illuminated in the years following Korea, it was primarily because the circumstances of this period did not put it sharply and clearly to the test. Not only did the nature of the threat seem clear, particularly in its relation to the world balance of power, but the direct and immediate relevance of the threat to American security went, on the whole, undisputed. Given these circumstances, America's Asian policy was supported for over a decade by what may be termed a negative consensus. The military commitments made by the Truman and Eisenhower administrations were maintained, though they evoked little enthusiasm. They also evoked little opposition so long as they did not entail a serious price. For a time, it was set forth as an official article of faith that these commitments would never entail a serious price, that is, a land war engaging American forces. There were many who did not share John Foster Dulles' confidence in the effectiveness as a deterrent to aggression of a "political warning system" for Asia, a system to be implemented primarily through collective defense arrangements and the threat of "selective retaliatory power." But so long as the Dulles system suffered no marked failure, it evoked no significant opposition.

Vietnam has finally put this negative consensus to the test and has laid bare its fragility. Moreover, the test has occurred in circumstances that cannot but illuminate the essential issue that has always provoked a disparity of view over America's Asian policy. The central circumstance, the circumstance that comprises, as it were, all other circumstances, is the substantial, one is tempted to say the radical, change in the structure of American security. There is, in fact, no meaningful comparison to be drawn between the security position of this nation in the late nineteen-forties and its security position today. Whereas in the nineteen-forties it was still entirely possible, if not entirely plausible, to imagine an imbalance of military power that would threaten the physical security of America, today this contingency is no longer a meaningful possibility. Whereas in the nineteen-forties it was still entirely possible, and altogether plausible, to imagine an imbalance of power resulting in a security problem the solution of which would severely strain the nation's resources and jeopardize its democratic institutions, today this contingency is, at best, very remote.

In part, this change in the structure of American security is the consequence of military-technological developments. Although nuclear-missile weapons have dealt a decisive blow to the territorial "impermeability" of the state, the security effects of these weapons have by no means been consistently negative. On the contrary, short of the extreme situation they have markedly improved the security problem for their possessors, at least if security is equated with physical security. If in the extreme situation the great nuclear power is indeed absolutely vulnerable vis-à-vis its great adversary, in other than extreme situations these same weapons render a great nuclear power physically secure to a degree that great powers seldom, if ever, enjoyed in the past. For the first time in history the prospect arises of a physical security that need no longer prove dependent on time-honored calculations of a balance of power. For the first time the prospect arises, if it has not already materialized, of a physical security no longer dependent on what transpires outside the North American continent.

In part, this change in the structure of American security is the consequence of economic and technological growth that has steadily widened the margin of power, at least in all forms other than strategic, between America and her nearest competitors, while markedly reducing the nation's economic dependence on the outside world. This growth has not resulted in conferring upon America a new status in the sixties that was not already enjoyed in the forties. What it has done is to consolidate and further strengthen the status of preponderant world power while exorcising the fears (and, for others, the hopes) of America's relative power decline that were widely entertained in the late fifties and even the early sixties. So full has the circle of men's expectations turned today that the degree of American preponderance is, if anything, exaggerated. Even so, the margin of power that is presently enjoyed, and the margin of power that is very likely to be enjoyed in the forseeable future, make it difficult to conjure up the vision of an imbalance of power resulting in a security problem whose solution would severely strain the nation's resources and jeopardize its democratic institutions.

In part, finally, this change in the structure of American security is the consequence of developments by now so apparent that they are mentioned only for the sake of formal completeness. The emergent, though still evolving, political and economic constellation of western Europe, the fragmentation and increasing state of disarray of the once vaunted communist bloc, the disruption of the Sino-Soviet alliance and the consequent moderation—for this and for other reasons—of Soviet policy, the ascendance of Japan to an economic position in Asia and in the world that is bound eventually to find a political and military expression more commensurate with this position—these and yet other developments have resulted in a Eurasia that bears only the faintest resemblance to the Eurasia of the late nineteen-forties. The great fear once entertained by American strategists, a fear which persisted into the postwar period, that a hostile power or combination of powers might succeed in uniting Eurasia and in turning its immense resources against the Western Hemisphere, can no longer be seriously entertained. What the dean of American diplomatic historians, a man noted for his sobriety, could seriously entertain in 1948—that the strategy of American security and defense would eventually have to be drawn in North America—can no longer be seriously entertained.[8]

---

[8] "What is the strategy of American security and defense now that collective security has failed and the balance of power has turned against us? It consists, I submit, in three lines of defense: a first line, in Europe; a second line, in the New World, south; a third line in the New World, north; along the Arctic Circle, perhaps south of it. That third line may become at any moment, the first line, in a new Pearl Harbor." Samuel Flagg Bemis, "The Shifting Strategy of American Defense and Diplomacy," *The Virginia Quarterly Review* (Summer 1948), p. 333. The view expressed in these

The measure of the change that has occurred in the structure of American security is strikingly illustrated in the contrast between the significance of containing the Soviet Union in the forties and the significance of containing China today. The early policy of containing the Soviet Union in Europe, as already observed, was more or less synonymous with a policy of the balance of power, and not merely with a regional balance of power but with the world balance. Obviously, if the Soviets had come to dominate western Europe they would have destroyed any semblance of a European balance of power. They would also have threatened, if not have overturned, the world balance. The equation of containing Soviet expansion in Europe, maintaining a regional and world balance of power and safeguarding the foundations of American security, was reasonably clear and persuasive. A similar equation in the case of China today is neither clear nor persuasive. What is the principal objective of America's Asian policy? Is it the containment of China or the maintenance of a balance of power? It will not do to answer that the two come to the same thing, for this is clearly not the case. At least, it is not so unless one piles tenuous and unverifiable assumption upon tenuous and unverifiable assumption respecting the indirect effects of Chinese expansion. In Asia, containment has no plausible relation to the world balance of power because the expansion of China in Asia cannot substantially affect that

---

lines is not at substantial variance with the view taken at the time by those charged with the conduct of American foreign policy. Cf. Joseph M. Jones, *The Fifteen Weeks* (1955).

balance. Even the containment of China and the maintenance of an Asian balance are not identical, unless we are to discount Soviet power to the west and north, dismiss the emergent power of Japan to the east, and neglect the power—if only naval and aerial—of the United States to the east and south. If, however, we take this power into consideration, it is apparent that a balance of power already exists in Asia, that it has existed for some time, and that China does not presently have, and cannot be expected to have in the near future, the power to overturn this balance. It is true that this balance cannot be relied upon to contain Chinese expansion to the south and southeast, though in the case of India it is possible that it may do so in the form of a tacit American-Soviet nuclear guarantee. But the expansion of China in the south, even if it were to take an overtly military form and to be entirely unimpeded (though neither of these contingencies is plausible), still cannot by itself decisively affect the Asian, let alone the world, balance of power. (The former balance could and surely would be altered, though very doubtfully the latter, only as a result of Chinese dominance over Japan.) The threat that Chinese expansion, or Chinese and North Vietnamese expansion, poses for American security differs not only quantitatively but qualitatively from the threat posed by Soviet expansion a generation ago.

This conclusion, with its obvious implications for American foreign policy, need not be accepted, especially if security is not limited to the nation's physical security as well as the integrity of its institutions. And even if security is so limited, it need not be accepted if the safety of the nation's institutions and, more generally, the quality of its domestic life are made dependent on the preservation, and the eventual realization, of these institutions elsewhere in the world. In turn, the preservation and the eventual realization of these institutions elsewhere in the world may be found to require a congenial world order, the creation and maintenance of which are deemed to be the awesome, though unavoidable, responsibilities of the nation. Through this simple reasoning a nation's security is made indistinguishable from a purpose or mission that encompasses all humanity, a purpose that gives to the nation's existence, hence its security, a potentially limitless dimension. A nation may preserve its body yet perish through the loss of its soul, or, what is made to appear virtually the same, the abandonment of its purpose. The nature of the security required by that purpose and by the responsibility for its faithful realization need bear little, if any, relation to the comparatively modest security that is merely a function of a balance of power. What to the latter is a peripheral interest, having little direct bearing on national security, to the former may be a vital interest, having the most intimate bearing on the nation's safety and welfare.

There is nothing new in the insistence upon identifying America's security with her purpose. That insistence is apparent in the Truman Doctrine, which, in turn, reflects a tradition that goes back to the very origins of American diplomacy. What is new are the lengths to which the identification of security and purpose has regularly been carried today by administration spokesmen. Nor will it do to dismiss expressions of this identification as mere rhetorical hyperbole ("We can be safe only to the extent that our total environment is safe"—Secretary of State Dean Rusk), for it is the very excessiveness of the terms in which the American security interest is presently cast that is significant and that requires explanation. Yet there is no mystery in what often appears to critics as an emphasis on security that is almost inversely proportional to the security interests at stake. Whereas in the late nineteen-forties America's purpose was a function of her security, in the late nineteen-sixties security has become a function of her purpose. It is precisely because security in its more conventional and limited sense is no longer of paramount concern that its importance is so emphasized. It is precisely because the nation is engaged in the vindication of other than, or more than, security interests that security is so emphasized. This emphasis, then, simply reflects an awareness that security continues to provide the principal, though of course not the only, justification for employing force, that the invocation of the security interests remains indispensable in order to sanction the costs of war. However great the emphasis placed on the larger purpose presumably informing American foreign policy, it still can not alone bear the burden of justifying the sacrifices entailed by the use of force. It can do so only if the nation's purpose is effectively equated with its security.

It is in the failure to make this equation effective that we must find the principal cause of domestic dissent over America's Asian policy. There are other factors that have significantly contributed to the dissent, not the least of which is the deep skepticism over the very meaning today of the American purpose abroad. They are still not comparable, however, to the apparent failure to equate security with purpose, whether in Vietnam or in Asia as a whole. Had the equation been effectively made, the frustration and distaste engendered by the Vietnamese war would never have achieved the proportions they did achieve. Had that equation been effectively made, the purely domestic sources of disaffection over Vietnam would never have been able to attain their present significance, despite the emergence of a domestic crisis whose severity and gravity we are only now beginning fully to appreciate. The significance of the debate is not that it raises the issue whether foreign or domestic policy ought to be primary, at least, not in a general sense. Instead, it raises the issue whether a certain kind of foreign policy ought to have primacy over domestic policy. It questions whether the primacy of foreign over domestic policy should continue to be affirmed on behalf of a policy that may involve the use of force to vindicate interests that, at best, are only indirectly related to the security of America (and that are increasingly held to have little relation even to the traditional purpose of America). At the root of the debate over American foreign policy is the fundamental question that has arisen for every nation which has achieved a certain degree of pre-eminence and relative freedom: nation or empire?

II. THE DEFENSE OF AMERICAN FOREIGN POLICY

It is not surprising that the relevance of this question—nation or empire?—is rejected by those who bear responsibility for the conduct of American foreign policy. Given the lengths to which professions of egalitarianism in international society have been carried today, the admission of imperial pretensions is out of the question. The universalization of the nation-state, consequent upon the dissolution of colonial empires, is held to yield a co-operative society of equals, not an imperial order of inequality. So seriously is this egalitarian ethos taken by most of the world today that it is no longer discreet for a great power even to admit to the role of policeman—contrary to the open professions of such a role during World War II—let alone to the more exalted status of imperial agent.

The new spirit is not uncongenial to the American tradition—at any rate, to the prevailing interpretation of this tradition—which is avowedly and emphatically anti-imperial. There are, of course, those historians who remind us that the Republic was commonly conceived by the Founding Fathers to be an "American Empire," that in its period of consolidation and early growth it manifested typical imperial strivings, that its continental expansion was an imperial expansion, and that its hemispheric policy—the other side of the same expansionist coin—has been an imperial policy.[1] On occasion, a

[1] Cf. R. W. Van Alstyne, *The Rising American Empire* (1960).

sharply revisionist historiography has even seen expansion as *the* principle of our institutions, though a principle that has been implemented, on the whole, through indirect methods of control.[2] Even so, the prevailing interpretation is otherwise. If the Founding Fathers spoke of an "American Empire" it was nevertheless to be a new kind of imperium, in Jefferson's sense of an "Empire of Liberty," distinguished by the nature of its growth and the principles of its organization as well as by its ultimate purpose. This imperium was conceived at the time of its origins as the very antithesis of the empires of the European states, which were based upon "reasons of state" and inspired by what Benjamin Franklin called the "pest of glory." If America was initially conceived as an empire, it was an empire destined by its very nature to be anti-imperial, an empire that was to promote the cause of freedom both in its domestic as well as in its foreign policies. Nor has our continental expansion been seen to detract from this image. To the extent that it was undertaken at the expense of European powers, it has of course appeared as the defeat of imperialism. To the extent that this expansion was undertaken at the expense of the indigenous population, it was still not imperialism because there were so few Indians (imperialism, in this view, begins with the millions not with the thousands, and with overseas territories not with contiguous territories). Our hemispheric policy has enjoyed an interpretation similar to our continental expansion. That this policy was designed to facilitate American expansion, hopefully over the whole of the North American continent, and

[2] William A. Williams, *The Tragedy of American Diplomacy* (rev. ed., 1962).

that it was rooted in security considerations which could be realized only by making the hemisphere an American sphere of influence, have not prevented us from interpreting the Monroe Doctrine as an historic blow struck against the imperial idea and as a vindication of the ideals of self-determination and self-government. In this traditional historiography the Truman Doctrine in our age applies to the world the principles embodied in the doctrine of Monroe, or, as one historian of American diplomacy has recently put it, the Truman Doctrine represents "the ultimate and logical conclusion of traditional American foreign policy."[3] That we have on occasion strayed from our anti-imperial commitment is not denied. What is denied is that these departures are more than aberrations, that they are more than exceptions, which in their infrequency and the moral embarrassment they have caused confirm an anti-imperial tradition.

Whatever the validity of this conventional interpretation of American diplomacy, there can be little doubt about the strength and persistence of our anti-imperial conviction and of the principal corollaries of this conviction. Perhaps no theme has been articulated more often by American statesmen than that the purposes and objectives of American foreign

[3] Francis L. Loewenheim, "A Legacy of Hope and a Legacy of Doubt," in Francis L. Loewenheim, ed., *The Historian and the Diplomat* (1967), p. 50. "There was . . . from the beginning of American history, a close and integral relationship between the idea of self-government, upon which the American Revolution was based, and the idea of national self-determination, with which it soon became closely connected, and which . . . has been the greatest contribution of the United States to the progress of international relations in modern times" (p. 7).

42

policy may be properly understood only as means to the end of protecting and promoting individual freedom and well-being. No end of foreign policy, not even the end of preserving the state's independence and survival, can be morally autonomous, self-justifying, an end in itself. Instead, all the ends of foreign policy must be viewed as means to the ends of society, which are in turn ultimately the ends of individuals. This need not and does not mean that domestic policy must have primacy over foreign policy. So long as the security and independence of the state are regarded as the indispensable means to the protection and promotion of individual and societal values, so long as the state remains the indispensable condition of values, there is necessarily a point at which foreign policy has primacy over domestic policy. It does mean that the principal purpose and justification of foreign policy is the promotion of domestic happiness and welfare. That purpose presumably must and does set important limits to foreign policy. Thus the rejection of the question we have posed—nation or empire?—seems to follow almost by definition the American tradition and purpose in foreign policy. "The American dream remains domestic," a former high official of the Kennedy and Johnson administrations writes, and adds: "Such inwardness of national feeling can be dangerous, but it has the enormously important consequence for others that the American democracy has no enduring taste for imperialism."[4]

If the question—nation or empire?—nevertheless persists, it does so both because its ultimate test is action rather than conviction and because that con-

[4] McGeorge Bundy, "The End of Either/Or," *Foreign Affairs* (January 1967), p. 189.

viction itself is not without ambivalence. Indeed, the element of conviction or purpose has always been ambivalent, at least in terms of its significance for policy. There has never been either a necessary or a self-evident relationship between commitment to the American purpose and commitment to a given foreign policy. The idea that there is such a relationship, that either a policy of isolationism or one of internationalism (or even one of interventionism) follows from the American purpose, has little basis in American history. The most disparate of policies apparently can be, and historically have been, reconciled with the nation's purpose. It is a commonplace that throughout America's history isolationists have only seldomly considered themselves to be truly isolationists. They have not rejected the American purpose or mission of bringing the blessings of freedom to all men, and not only Americans; they have only insisted that this purpose must be achieved in a certain manner, that is, through a policy of nonentanglement. But nonentanglement from the very start encompassed an idea of "national duty," a duty to be served by, and implemented through, the power of moral example. The mission of regenerating the world and the isolationist impulse were seldom seen as contradictory. Instead, both arose from the central conviction of the unique character and absolute significance of our experience.[5]

To say that both isolationist and interventionist impulses are rooted in the American purpose, and

[5] "We have been able to dream of ourselves as emancipators of the world at the very moment that we have withdrawn from it. We have been able to see ourselves as saviors at the very moment that we have been isolationists." Louis Hartz, *The Liberal Tradition in America* (1955), p. 38.

that both an isolationist and an interventionist policy may be reconciled with this purpose, is not to deny the obvious and important differences between the two. Although both impulses may have a common spiritual root, and both policies may be encompassed by the same purpose, it is still a matter of enormous importance which impulse and which policy prevail. In less categorical terms, what kind of compromise is reached between these two radical alternatives is enormously important. The nature of that compromise, the manner in which the American purpose is to be sought, has been a critical issue in nearly every great debate over American foreign policy since the beginning of the Republic. It is the larger issue raised by Vietnam, however seldom it is explicitly raised. Not only is it the larger issue raised by the present debate, circumstances have permitted the issue to assume a form it could not assume in the past. Whereas in the past, including even the recent past, America's position in the international system placed relatively narrow limits on the manner in which this issue would—and could —be resolved, America's present position has dramatically broadened the spectrum of possible solutions. At least, this is so if we assume that greater power confers greater freedom (admittedly an assumption the powerful have never been disposed to accept).[6]

The point may be put more sharply. The significance of the recurring debate over the means of

[6] To be sure, one of the criticisms of American foreign policy is precisely the assumption of a greater degree of freedom than political realities warrant. Whatever the validity of this criticism, it does not affect the above point— unless we are to assume that what has hitherto been the normal order of affairs among men and nations has now been radically reversed.

realizing the American purpose cannot usefully be considered apart from the circumstances surrounding the debate. In an earlier period, the circumstances attending this debate necessarily served to limit its scope and significance. If America was secure throughout the nineteenth century, her power relative to the power of others was still distinctly limited. In the present century, the steady growth of American power relative to the power of others has led to, and even forced, an almost continuing debate over the American purpose and how best to realize it. It is only in the face of a substantial threat to American security, narrowly conceived, that the debate over purpose has diminished in significance. Given the apparent recession of that threat concomitant with the sudden appreciation—perhaps the overappreciation—of America's preponderance, an issue never resolved has once again arisen and in a form it could never before assume. For the first time, circumstances permit the nation to come, as it were, face to face with its purpose, because for the first time circumstances no longer seem to place narrow limits on the means by which this purpose may be pursued.

What is relevant here is not the preferable solution to a traditional problem. It is the recognition that our overweening sense of purpose is one of the distinguishing marks of an imperial power. That this sense of purpose may be expressed, and in an earlier period was expressed, by a policy of isolation indicates its ambivalence for action, in part according to circumstance, not its inherently anti-imperial character. That the principal tenet of this purpose is avowedly anti-imperial does not preclude the pursuit of goals which, again according to the circumstances, may nevertheless result in imperial relationships. America would not be the first power that pursued an imperial policy under the banner of anti-imperialism. Nor is it sufficient when dismissing the relevance of the question—nation or empire?—simply to reaffirm that the American dream remains domestic. If there is necessarily a point—for America as for all nations—at which foreign policy has primacy over domestic policy, the all-important issue is the manner in which the security requirements of the nation are conceived. It may well be true that so long as security is conceived in a traditional and restricted manner, as a function of the balance of power, the ultimate primacy of foreign over domestic policy need not detract significantly from the normal order of things in which domestic happiness and welfare are primary. This is particularly so for states which, by virtue of relative power and geography, enjoy a highly favorable measure of security. Even for such fortunate states, however, the commitment in principle to the primacy of domestic over foreign policy may mean little in practice if security is achieved only when, in the words of Secretary of State Rusk, "the total environment is safe." If security is interpreted as a function both of a favorable balance of power between states and of the internal order maintained by states, that is, as a favorable ideological balance of power, foreign policy may have primacy over domestic policy in a way that is all-pervasive.

It is, then, the insistence upon defining American security in terms of a purpose beyond conventional security requirements that reinforces the significance of that purpose as a national interest which may prove indistinguishable from an imperial interest.

It is the insistence upon defining American security both in terms of the international relations of states, though even this definition has been very broad, and in terms of the internal nature of their politics that may readily transform a national interest into an imperial interest. If such a transformation is increasingly apparent today, it did not spring full-blown from the Johnson administration, though this administration has surely made its contribution to an imperial America. There is no basis, however, for the curious and persistent belief that in doing so President Johnson has deviated from a course set by his predecessors, and particularly his immediate predecessor. In principle, President Kennedy was no less interventionist and no less interventionist in pursuit of a common purpose. It is true that Kennedy found a new way of articulating that purpose. In his now famous address at American University on June 10, 1963, he declared: "If we cannot end now our differences, at least we can help make the world safe for diversity." And in an earlier State of the Union address, he had observed: " . . . our basic goal remains the same: a peaceful world community of free and independent states, free to choose their own future and their own system so long as it does not threaten the freedom of others. Some may choose forms and ways that we would not choose for ourselves, but it is not for us that they are choosing." These are the principal expressions relied upon by those who would argue that Kennedy represented a departure, however short-lived, from the messianic drive to universalize freedom proclaimed in the Truman Doctrine. Yet there is no real disparity between them and the expression of purpose in the Truman Doctrine. The Truman Doctrine did not

license intervention on behalf of the cause of freedom so long as that cause was not threatened by
aggression from without or by armed minorities
from within. To this extent Kennedy's statements
are no different from what his predecessors and
successor have insisted on retaining. Nor do they
suggest the abandonment of the conviction that
others will choose as we have chosen, if not now,
then eventually. If they suggest a modest change
of emphasis and of tone, it can be explained, apart
from personal style, largely in terms of the circumstances of the time. The appreciation of diversity
came at the end of a period in which America's
principal adversary had failed to realize its aspiration to parity, let alone to supremacy. Moreover,
the sudden realization of America's preponderance
was attended by the open and almost complete rup-
ture of relations between the Soviet Union and
China. The emphasis on diversity was borne of and
reflected the newly found and growing confidence
that things were going our way. A détente with the
Soviet Union, however modest in character, would
of necessity have to be based on the implicit recognition of America's preponderance. In turn, the acceptance of this preponderance by the Soviet Union
was not only entirely compatible with the principle
of diversity but made such acceptance somewhat
more palatable. Given a world in which America
was preponderant, and likely to remain so, diversity
represented not so much a departure from, as an
expedient and felicitous formulation of, a traditional
aspiration. Even a diverse world was still expected
to be a world moving steadily in the direction of
freedom. And even to make the world safe for

diversity a national interest, conventionally defined, would prove insufficient.

The transformation of a national interest into one of imperial dimension need not be marked by any clear break, whether in word or in action. In word, interests may continue to be expressed in terms of an unchanging purpose, which, however, may only serve to veil the reality of changing interests. And if the nature of interests is revealed through action rather than expression of purpose, through power rather than ideology, difficulties may still persist in distinguishing between nation and empire. These difficulties result not so much from differences over what constitutes the general characteristics of an imperium as from differences over the proper identification in practice of characteristics that are commonly acknowledged. An imperial state is distinguished by magnitude of power, scope and nature of purpose, and the character of its relationships with other states. The requirement of power is obvious, though the magnitude of power required for imperial status may be less than clear. The requirement of purpose is equally apparent, though its distinctiveness in identifying the imperial state may be less than apparent. An imperial state, by definition, must have as its purpose the creation and maintenance of order. For the relationships of control maintained with other, and weaker, states are constitutive of order. This order-creating and maintaining purpose, however, will characterize great—though less than imperial—states as well. If there is a distinction here, it must be found in the scope afforded to, rather than the nature of, this purpose and, of course, in the freedom with which it is defined and implemented. Yet the scope of purpose, and freedom in definition and implementation, like magnitude of power, are matters of degree. Finally, although the existence of order necessarily implies relationships of control, the manner of control is clearly one of degree. In this respect, as in others, there may be no clear distinction between the imperial and the less-than-imperial state. Nor does it advance matters to say that the kinds of control exercised by an imperial state must be intended to prevent action threatening to or destructive of a given order, for this is implicit in the very concept of order, whoever maintains it and whatever the specific form it may take.

These considerations indicate both that the distinction between nation and empire is one of degree and that the imperial state is, as it were, the realization of aspirations already apparent in less-than-imperial states. Thus the identification of the imperial state, and of those values presumably represented by it, with a potentially universal community is but a manifestation of a general tendency of states to identify the collective self with something larger than the self. Indeed, the progressive extension of the collective self, and consequently the progressive extension of perceived threats to that self, form part of the "natural history" of all great nations. The greater the power of the collective self the greater the dimensions imputed to the collective's existence beyond the merely physical dimension. The greater the power of nations, the more expansively they come to view their "necessities," or, to employ a more common euphemism, their "responsibilities." The cynic will therefore conclude, and not without reason, that power creates interests—the latter expanding in rough proportion

51

to the former—which are then seen as necessities or responsibilities.[7] In any case, the insistence of imperial powers on identifying themselves with a universal—or potentially universal—community is almost invariable. It is neither accidental nor mysterious, then, that imperial states almost invariably refuse to distinguish between the security of the imperial state and the security of the greater community.

Whether this process is indeed determined, whether it occurs quite independently of men's will, need not be dealt with here. A positive response would of course make the question—nation or empire?—meaningless. All that would remain for meaningful argument and choice would be the nature of the empire or the kind of imperial order. Few seem to believe that this is all that remains, including those who have most insistently urged an imperial America or, rather, who have urged a more consistent, self-assured, and successful imperial America. It is true, however, that if America is not irrevocably committed by her power and her purpose to be an imperial state that she is one at the present time. And it is this new role that must largely account for the apparent inability of the Johnson administration to present a persuasive rationale for the war in Vietnam. There is a logic to the arguments

[7] This conclusion of the cynic may be overdrawn. It is worth emphasis, however, if only as a correction of the widespread view that men's interests somehow arise independently, or almost so, of their power. The latter view is reflected in the current demand that we must first consider our interests and then determine whether or not we have the power sufficient to realize these interests. Unfortunately, the normal process—some will say the "natural" process— seems to be almost the reverse.

urged in defense of the war and, more generally, of Asian policy as a whole, but it is not the logic of past arguments. If the change that has occurred is obscured this is due, in part, to the apparent ease with which the American purpose can be reconciled with very disparate policies, including an imperial policy. In part, however, this is a result of the striking, and paradoxical, similarity in the security arguments that may be invoked on behalf of nation as well as of empire. The view that these arguments must differ substantially, that their structure must prove clearly dissimilar, is unfounded. Although the object to be secured differs, if in the one case it is a nation and in the other an empire, the form of the argument nevertheless remains essentially unchanged. It is not the form but the meaning of the argument that has changed. The defense of American foreign policy today is no longer a defense of national security and interests but of imperial security and interests. The failure to apprehend this on the part of the public and the unwillingness—perhaps partly unconscious—to acknowledge this on the part of the administration are at the root of the present public confusion and malaise.

In its essential form the rationale of American foreign policy has remained unchanged since World War II. This rationale is based on a vision of world order—a vision that embodies the American purpose —the principal elements of which were set forth in the Truman Doctrine. There is an apparent simplicity about the American vision of world order that readily lends it to caricature, and, indeed, its simplicity is perhaps its most striking characteristic. Reiterated on innumerable occasions, its basic requirements are, to cite a recent expression of them, "that acts of aggression and breaches of the peace have to be suppressed, that disputes ought to be settled by peaceful means, that the basic human rights ought to be sustained, and that governments must cooperate across their frontiers in the great humanitarian purposes of all mankind." In these words of Secretary of State Dean Rusk, words that have formed an almost invariable preface to any of his general pronouncements on the nation's foreign policy or the meaning of the war in Vietnam, critics have come to see something intrinsically unserious. But if Secretary Rusk has been unserious in his statements, then the same must be said of every Secretary of State and President over the past generation.[8]

Any concept of order, including the time-honored concept of an order of balanced power, must be cast in general terms. It is not a valid criticism of the American concept of world order to point out that it partakes of great generalities. None of its principal exponents has assumed that these gen-

[8] And not only the past generation, though this is the period with which we are concerned. In its last note to Japan (November 26, 1941), preceding the outbreak of war in the Pacific, the United States outlined the possible basis of an agreement with Japan in terms of the following principles: "(1) The principle of inviolability of territorial integrity and sovereignty of each and all nations. (2) The principle of noninterference in the internal affairs of other countries. (3) The principle of equality, including equality of commercial opportunity and treatment. (4) The principle of reliance upon international cooperation and conciliation for the prevention and pacific settlement of controversies and for improvement of international conditions by peaceful methods and processes." These principles are little more than a paraphrase of the principles set forth by Woodrow Wilson in World War I.

eralities could provide, in and of themselves, a sufficient guide to action, or that they could be applied without regard to the particular circumstances attending, and invariably limiting, their application. None has assumed that these principles could be sought independently of the existing distribution of power, though few have been willing to acknowledge the scope of potential conflict between requirements of principle and requirements of power. Finally, none has assumed a correspondence between postulated order and political reality, a correspondence which would make the pursuit of order superfluous. What has been assumed is both the desirability of these great generalities as goals and the necessity of seeking them in order to maintain an environment in which freedom in America could and would be assured.

The first and foremost principle for maintaining such an environment is that aggression shall not be resorted to, that states shall not use armed force or the threat of armed force save as a legitimate measure of self- or collective defense against armed attack. This preoccupation with proscribing the resort to force is not qualified by the nature of the causes that might have prompted the initiation of force. Whatever the nature of these causes, they are not regarded as providing a justification for the initiation of force; whatever a state's grievances, they are not regarded as sanctioning the resort to aggression. If the principle has not been applied with a fine consistency and impartiality to allies, neutrals, and adversaries alike, it has nevertheless been applied to allies—as in 1956 to Great Britain and France over Suez—and to neutrals—as in 1961 to India over Goa. Understandably, consistency of application is higher in the case of adversaries who are considered to represent the principal threat to order. The central issues at stake in Vietnam, administration officials have insisted throughout the war, are how the peace of the world is to be organized and whether America is to use its influence and power to prevent the resort to aggression (thereby protecting the right to self-determination and to independence). These have presumably been the central issues at stake in all of the major confrontations America has had with communist powers since the outset of the cold war.

Although the first and foremost principle comprising the American concept of world order is the proscription of the aggressive use of force, that concept is not equated with an order in which peace, conceived simply as the absence of force, may be founded on injustice. Peace is not acknowledged, at least not consciously, as a higher value than justice; the vision of world order we have sought is not equated with the status quo, any status quo, however unjust. Nor has the security of states been conceived only in terms of protection against the open and direct use of force. Instead, peace and justice have been considered as two sides of the same coin, and security has been conceived in terms considerably broader than protection against the overt resort to force. If the difficulties inherent in this attempted reconciliation have been acknowledged only seldom, it is largely because of the persistence of the conviction that states need not resort to force either to secure justice or to insure their security, that there are no conflicts of interest so intractable that force will appear as the only solution, and that when collectives do resort to force

56

they choose a course of action they might—and, therefore, should—have avoided. The insistence on condemning the initiation of force does not spring simply from moral aversion to the methods of violence as well as from the belief that these methods are destructive of order, but from the traditional American interpretation of conflict, in which aggression is not only an evil but an unnecessary evil.

This interpretation extends, as well, to forms of conflict which fall short of armed force. The American vision of an international order characterized by cooperation rather than conflict, and based upon the principles of equality and consent rather than hierarchy and coercion, is not simply held out as an ideal to be striven after. Instead, the ideal is considered almost as the "natural" condition, and the antagonisms and conflicts among nations are viewed as a departure from the normal state of affairs.[9] But although the American concept of international order is regarded as immanent, in the sense that the intrinsic justice of the principles on which it is based are regarded as self-evident, the realization of this order obviously remains an aspiration, not a fact. In the real world, conflict and antagonism are acknowledged, however reluctantly. Nevertheless, and this is the significant point, the distinction remains between conflict carried on by

[9] Twenty years ago Walter Lippmann wrote of our "refusal to recognize, to admit, to take as the premise of our thinking, the fact that rivalry and strife and conflict among states, communities, and factions are the normal conditions of mankind. . . . In the American ideology the struggle for existence, and the rivalry for advantages, are held to be wrong, abnormal, and transitory. . . ." "The Rivalry of Nations," *The Atlantic Monthly* (February 1948), p. 18.

methods short of armed force and conflict pursued by armed force.

Given the optimistic view that force need never be employed aggressively, the dilemma of choosing between peace and the preservation of other interests should never arise. In fact, it does arise and must arise, even for America, as the successive policies of containing communism—Russian, Chinese, Cuban, North Vietnamese—have shown. In part, that dilemma has been resolved—or perhaps spirited away—by the belief that peace, conceived simply as the absence of armed force, forms the necessary and sufficient condition for the realization of these other interests. Policies of containment have reflected the belief that the changes which would occur if force were not resorted to would be of a certain character, that these changes would conform to our interests as a nation and prove compatible with our vision of international order. In part, however, that dilemma has been resolved by interpreting the prohibition on force so as to fit the requirements of containment policies. This task was facilitated from the start by the view that what constitutes aggression, or even an armed attack, is not at all self-evident, and that care must be exercised to avoid imputing too great a rigidity to this standard. Thus the prohibition on force has not been interpreted as precluding application of the concept of aggression or armed attack to situations in which internal revolutions are supported in varying degree by outside powers. Four successive administrations have been committed to the position that at least certain forms of "indirect aggression" might be assimilated to the concept of armed attack, thereby justifying the resort to force as a measure of self- or collective

58

defense, though the nature of the circumstances in which indirect aggression may be held to justify the use of force remains as obscure today as at the outset of Soviet-American rivalry.

These considerations, taken together with inconsistency of application and even the open disregard of principle, have led many critics to conclude that, far from providing a foundation for international order, the principle is scarcely distinguishable from mere ideology, whose purpose is to provide a spurious justification for almost any use of force.[10] America has neither actively opposed nor even verbally condemned all armed aggression. More important are those occasions in which America has resorted to the aggressive use of force, whether directly or indirectly. The American organization and support of armed intervention in 1961 against the government of Cuba, however abortive the result, was at the very least a case of indirect aggression. The forcible measures initiated by the United States in 1962, in response to the discovery that the Soviet Union was secretly establishing missile sites on the island of Cuba, were not justified as measures of legitimate self-defense and, in any event, could only have been so justified with considerable difficulty. The American intervention in the Dominican Republic in 1965 was not taken in response to an act of aggression, direct or indirect. Nor is the aggressive character of that intervention substantially affected by the fact that it received,

[10] Distinguish this criticism from the criticism that in asserting what is in effect the right of an international police power America has become a counter-revolutionary state and not merely with respect to Communist revolutions but to all attempts to change the status quo by force.

though only under American pressure and at the last moment, the collective sanction of the Inter-American states. Moreover, on each of these occasions we have not only resorted to the aggressive use of force but have asserted a right to do so if, in the judgment of the American government, the security interests of this nation were deemed to require forcible intervention.

Is the conclusion justified, then, that the first and foremost principle comprising the American concept of world order is no more than ideology? It would not seem so. What the above considerations do clearly indicate, apart from the inevitable bias attending state action, is the almost insuperable difficulty, given the nature of international society, of consistently reconciling the principle forbidding the resort to force with the preservation of other interests. However much that difficulty may be denied in thought, in the absence of an effective political order, it cannot be denied in practice if other interests are to be preserved. For the restraints placed on the use of force cannot alone constitute an effective political order which may be relied upon to preserve other interests. These restraints are rather the expression of a certain scheme or method for the organization of power. Whether that scheme will give rise to an effective order cannot be determined simply by analyzing the nature of the restraints placed on force. It must be determined instead by examining the character of political reality and by comparing this reality with the nature of the restraints which are intended to regulate it. When this is done, the difficulty becomes apparent. Whereas the proscription on force in the American concept of world order presupposes a political reality that has never existed in international society, American policy has responded to a political reality that has required occasional departure from principle if interests other than peace were to be preserved. Of this, the successive policies of containment may be seen to provide a general illustration and the Cuban missile crisis a particular illustration. The governing requirement of containment, whether of the Soviet Union or of China, has been that a hostile power must not be allowed to expand, whatever the methods of expansion. In this sense, containment has sought to create and to maintain an order, not by the methods and restraints of the United Nations Charter, but by the traditional methods of countering hostile and expansionist Powers with power. That these methods cannot always be restricted by the principle proscribing initial resort to force was given dramatic and illuminating illustration in the Cuban missile crisis.

The nature of international society therefore makes a disparity between principle and practice inevitable.[11] It is inevitable in America's case if only

[11] Given the nature of international society, the disparity between principle and practice must have other manifestations as well. Among the more significant is the profession of equality and the reality of inequality (hence of hierarchy and special privilege). Whereas the profession of equality requires multilateral action, the reality of inequality leads—as always—to unilateral action. This disparity finds a reflection, an important reflection, in the persistence with which the concept of "spheres of influence" is rejected and the idea of "regionalism" is championed in American foreign policy. Whereas spheres of influence are based on hierarchy, regionalism is presumably based on equality; whereas spheres of influence are coercive arrangements, and largely unilateral, regionalism is presumably based on consent and multilateralism. The limits on "regionalism" in the Western Hemisphere are a matter of historic record.

for the reason that peace—the absence of force—is not the only interest of American policy and the proscription of force not the only principle of the American concept of world order. Indeed, the attempt consistently to reconcile the principle proscribing force and practice must prove especially difficult for America precisely because of the other interests of policy, above all the interest in universalizing freedom. To be sure, a concept of world order indifferent to the internal character of the states would not thereby do away with the difficulties arising from a general proscription on the resort to force. But it would at least reduce these difficulties insofar as it would confine them to challenges, however such challenges might arise, to the international balance of power (challenges which might initially arise through regional imbalances). For the great nuclear powers such challenges to their security, restrictively defined, are likely to prove increasingly rare. These considerations are evidently inapplicable, however, where security is equated, in large measure, with the "internal balance" and the presumed necessity of preventing unfavorable changes in this balance. They are evidently inapplicable where a concept of world order comprises the principle that the right of self-determination must also imply the right of self-government.

The dilemma—indeed, the inner contradiction—implicit in a concept of world order that comprises these two central principles may be resolved, if only on the level of thought, by the optimistic assumption that enforcement of the one principle—proscribing aggression, whether direct or indirect—will necessarily result in the realization of the other principle—societies based on, or moving in the direction of,

consent. In fact, that assumption has never been sub-
scribed to without qualification and, consequently, the
dilemma has never really been resolved. The Truman
Doctrine sought to harmonize the two principles and
to relate both to American security, which was in
turn equated with international order: "Totalitarian
regimes imposed on free peoples, by direct or indirect
aggression, undermine the foundations of international peace and hence the security of the United
States." Yet the qualifications placed on this seeming
harmony are readily apparent in the statement that
"it must be the policy of the United States to support
free peoples who are resisting attempted subjugation
by armed minorities or by outside pressures." There
is no limitation here to afford support only in the
event armed minorities are given assistance by an
external power. Nor is there a limitation on the
kind of support that may be afforded "free peoples"
resisting attempted subjugation by "armed minorities."

Thus the historic statement that marks the great
transformation in American foreign policy reveals
as clearly as does any subsequent statement the possible contradiction between the commitment to the
cause of freedom and the commitment to abstain
from forcible intervention in the internal affairs of
states. Nor is this qualification removed by substitut-
ing the principle of diversity for the principle of
freedom. For the principle of diversity, as earlier
observed, represents little more than a sophisticated
version of the principle of freedom proclaimed in
the Truman Doctrine. The principle of diversity was
not interpreted simply as the right of every people
to make a free choice regarding their government
if the effect was a government that then foreclosed

the right to make a free choice. Instead, that principle was interpreted as requiring the retention of the right to free choice, a right that must evidently have little meaning unless it is attended by the institutions of democratic government. So interpreted, the principle of diversity is in substance scarcely distinguishable from the principle of freedom, and the cause of diversity scarcely distinguishable from the cause of freedom.[12] The dilemma implicit in the Truman Doctrine therefore remains unchanged and unresolved.

The difficulties inherent in the American concept of world order have been equally inherent, and apparent, in the principal policy expression of this order—containment. If these difficulties have not prevented the rationalization and even the implementation of policy, at least if they have not done so in

[12] For a different view of President Kennedy's "world safe for diversity," see Paul Seabury, *The Rise and Decline of the Cold War* (1967). Seabury finds in Kennedy's outlook a subtle transformation of the cause of freedom into the cause of diversity. Of the latter he writes: "Proclaimed by a hegemonic power such as America, it required a degree of self-restraint and a reduction in the degree of American liberal interest in the internal affairs of other nations" (p. 53). This view is difficult to accept, however, since it is not borne out either by the interpretation given to the cause of diversity or by the actions of the Kennedy administration. Moreover, the principle of free choice was never left unqualified, even as interpreted in the text above. For Kennedy, social and political change, even if carried out by free choice, must not involve the prestige or commitments of America and Russia or upset the balance of power. Thus the Castro regime was not so much objectionable because it had gained and held power undemocratically, but because it offered Soviet communism a base in the Western Hemisphere, because it constituted a hostile government in the area of American vital interest.

the past, it is because they have always been qualified by the conviction that communism—whether monolithic or polycentric—provided the principal and, indeed, the only substantive threat to world order. It is this conviction that gives an apparent consistency to what would otherwise appear as inconsistent. It is this conviction, and the actions to which it has led, that gives concrete meaning to what would otherwise appear as an abstract scheme without tangible relation to the realities of power. And it is the same conviction that permits justifying the neglect and even the occasional open disregard of professed principles as not subversive of an order comprising those principles.

What is relevant here is not the validity of this conviction, since obviously it is valid in that if there has been and remains today a serious threat to the American concept of world order, and consequently the realization of the American purpose, that threat must stem from the existence of communist powers. The relevant point is the insistence with which, and the manner in which, successive administrations, and particularly the Johnson administration, have identified the preservation—or the progressive realization—of this concept of world order and American security. Equally relevant are the consequences to which the identification has led, above all in Vietnam.

The insistence on equating world order and American security is a matter of notoriety and need not be labored. It is worth noting, though, that the insistence on this identification marks every official effort to rationalize American foreign policy. It also marks almost every unofficial effort, however sophisticated and elaborate the latter may be. Whether projected in immediate or in long-range terms, whether made explicit or merely implicit, whether related directly to traditional purpose or considered separately from purpose, that identification forms the nerve root of efforts to vindicate American foreign policy. If the insistence is more pronounced today than in the recent past, the reason must be found, as already suggested, in the changes that have occurred over twenty years in the structure of American security. If these changes have resulted in a dramatic improvement in the security of the nation, they have not lessened the need to justify policy—above all, the need to justify the threat or use of force—largely in terms of security. This being so, the tendency to identify the nation's security with the maintenance of world order assumes almost the character of a compulsion. For it is only by virtue of this identification that the plea of security can be made plausible. Without this identification the policy of containment in Asia is deprived of its principal sanction. Without this identification the American alliance system as a whole can no longer be justified on grounds that initially provided its principal justification.

Thus it is not surprising that the policy of containment in Asia today is interpreted as the lineal descendant of the policy of containment in Europe and that both are found to serve the same vital interests and to further the same over-all purpose of achieving and maintaining a desirable world order. Nor is it surprising that the principal instrument of containment (apart, of course, from American power itself), the American alliance system, is still regarded as the vital ligament of world order, the continued integrity of which forms an indispensable condition of American security. In this view, the decisive issues are not whether the circumstances attending a policy of containment in Asia are different from those in Europe, since they obviously are very different, but the reasons for undertaking containment yesterday in Europe and today in Asia. These reasons, it is asserted, remain essentially the same. The threat to world order, hence to American security, may be more subtle and complex today than the threat of twenty years ago, but it is not less real. Failure to oppose, by whatever means necessary, the forcible expansion of Asian communism—whether Chinese or North Vietnamese—will jeopardize the entire structure of world order so painfully constructed over two decades.

Why is it, then, that this persisting threat is not more commonly appreciated? If the containment of communism in an earlier period elicited broad support, why is it that the containment of Asian communism today has failed to do so? In the main,[13] the answer given by the administration and its supporters is that the conditions of American security are more difficult to perceive today. And they are presumably more difficult to perceive because they no longer take a familiar form. Containment in Europe was initially undertaken in response to conditions whose meaning for American security was readily apparent, or very nearly so. Containment in Europe was undertaken primarily to prevent an im-

---

[13] I say in the main since there are other factors that are held up to account for this apparent lack of wide-spread support—a general weariness with external concerns, a growing concern with domestic problems, etc. The issue, however, is one of the relative priority or significance of the factors that deprive Asian containment of the broad support enjoyed by its predecessor.

balance of power, an imbalance that was seen at the time, and an imbalance that experience had enabled men to see at the time, as threatening American security in the direct and conventional sense. The same perceived threat to Europe and, consequently, to the world balance of power, afforded the basis for, and gave support to, the initial extension of containment to Asia. The difficulty of containment in Asia today—apart from the admittedly distasteful and frustrating features that mark the war in Vietnam—is therefore attributed to conditions of security that are unfamiliar, conditions that experience has not enabled men clearly to perceive, if at all.

The change in the geographical center of gravity of American foreign policy does not account for this failure of perception, though conventional wisdom had decreed that American security could be threatened only by an imbalance of power centered in Europe, not an imbalance in Asia alone. To be sure, an imbalance of power in Asia is held to represent, in and of itself, a threat to American security. But the principal threat to American security, it is argued, can neither be confined to Asia nor understood simply in conventional balance of power terms with its emphasis upon parity or superiority in material power. Instead, it must be found in the temptation afforded adversary states in Asia and elsewhere, consequent upon an American failure to deter communist aggression, to challenge the entire structure of world order that American policy has sought to create and maintain in the post-World War II period and to do so by means which must ultimately—and inevitably—raise the danger of nuclear war. That this challenge would not be decentralized would not diminish the threat to American security. Whether communism is monolithic or pluralistic is not an argument on which all else can be made to depend. For the significance that is so regularly attached by administration critics to the present division of the major communist powers would prove compelling only if security were still to be understood in traditional, prenuclear, terms. As between nuclear powers, however, if we are to speak of a balance of power at all, that balance must be understood not primarily in material terms but in psychological terms, not upon a structure of material power and therefore relative material advantage, but upon a structure of deterrent threat. There is no way to maintain the credibility and integrity of a deterrent threat save by manifesting a willingness to oppose forcible communist expansion, particularly when directed against an ally, and this even though such expansion is directly undertaken—indeed, independently undertaken—by a small communist state. For the deterrence of other, and larger, potential aggressors, however disunited, is dependent on the deterrence of all aggressors. It is the failure, then, to grasp the changed meaning of security today that must account for the misplaced emphasis critics insist upon attaching to the fact that communism is no longer monolithic.

These considerations also explain the insistence that the American alliance system is still the vital ligament of world order, whose continued integrity forms an indispensable condition of the nation's security. In this view, it is not decisive that the conditions attending the construction of the system no longer obtain. Critics may point out that whereas in the late nineteen-forties an independent Europe, allied to the United States, formed an essential condition of U.S. security, this is no longer clearly the case; that whereas even in the late nineteen-fifties the strategic bases provided by allies in Europe and Asia formed an indispensable element of American security, in the late nineteen-sixties these bases have become dispensable; and that whereas no marked disparity between motivation and rationale characterized alliance policy in an earlier period, such a disparity is bound to characterize alliance policy today since the purpose of this policy has changed from one of providing added and needed security to one of providing a manifestation of great power status and a means—though a means not always effective—of insuring great power control. The answers to this criticism are that it fails to appreciate the security significance of American alliance policy today and that it partially misinterprets the purpose and significance of this policy in an earlier period. Thus it is argued that even in an earlier period the purpose and significance of American alliance policy were not restricted to security considerations, narrowly and conventionally conceived. To the extent that alliance policy has reflected the more general policy of containment, it has also shared the same interests as containment, which were never narrowly conceived. If the conditions in which the American alliance system was constructed have changed, the interest in world order this system reflects—and is, indeed, very nearly synonymous with—nevertheless remains. Moreover, that interest in world order cannot be considered today apart from American security. That critics do so is due, once again, to their assumption, however inarticulate and even unconscious, that security must still be seen in the conventional terms of a balance of power. But once this assumption is rejected, as it must be rejected, it will be seen that the alleged changes in purpose and significance of the American alliance system are only apparent. The integrity of this system therefore remains as important today for world order and American security as it has ever been. To fail to defend any one of the component parts of the system is to jeopardize the whole. To jeopardize the whole is inevitably to incur the danger of a nuclear conflict.

The conviction that world order forms an undifferentiated whole, that a challenge by a communist power to one part of this order is a challenge to every part, not only accounts for the corollary conviction that peace is indivisible, it also explains the largely undifferentiated character of interests in American foreign policy. Traditional statecraft takes as axiomatic the need to differentiate interests, to distinguish between more or less important interests, between interests for which war is to be risked and for which war is not to be risked, or between interests for which a limited use of force appears justified and interests for which almost any use of force appears justified. For nations, as for individuals, the need to grade interests, however roughly, seems so apparent, so much a part of the natural scheme of things, that its bare acknowledgment is almost redundant. For nations, as for individuals, the need to pick and choose among objects that are desired according to the value imputed to these objects (which is, in turn, nearly always a function of their cost), appears as one of the prerequisites of rational behavior. To say this is not to say that there is a rational, and objectively valid, scheme for distinguishing and for grading interests in order of importance or desirability. There is no rational method for determining whether a nation should choose security for the future rather than glory for the present. It does not follow, however, that because all interests are ultimately subjective they are, as a matter of practical judgment, thereby equal in worth. The ultimate subjectivity of interests is a philosophical proposition. It does not affect either the practical need to distinguish and to grade interests or the possibility of doing so by resort to standards formed from experience and informed by prudential judgment. That some interests are objectively more important than others may not be a valid proposition of philosophy, but it is clearly a valid proposition of statecraft.

Nor is the need to distinguish and to grade interests affected by their interdependence. That interests are interdependent, or interconnected, is undoubtedly true. It does not follow, however, that because interests are interdependent they therefore form an undifferentiated whole. What follows is their ultimate—or residual—indeterminacy, an indeterminacy that is apparent in the difficulty of calculating the price entailed in preserving—or sacrificing—a given interest. This indeterminacy is one of the principal, and perennial, uncertainties of statecraft. Yet its acknowledgment does not and cannot affect the need to distinguish and to order interests.

American foreign policy does not and cannot entirely deny this elementary need. At the same time, the insistence with which the American conception of world order is seen as an undifferentiated whole, identified with American security, does clearly militate toward such denial. If it is once accepted that all parts are interdependent, then each part is, for all practical purposes, equally important. The consistency with which the "domino effect" has been invoked in every major, and minor, crisis of American foreign policy from President Truman's request in 1947 for aid to Greece and Turkey to the present war in Vietnam cannot be attributed simply to the need for exaggeration in order to obtain public support for foreign policy initiatives. In large measure, the invocation of that effect must be attributed to the conviction that to pick and choose the circumstances of American opposition to communist aggression, according to some arbitrary scheme of the relative importance of the interests involved, would be to jeopardize the whole fabric of international order upon which American security depends. The insistence on the indivisibility of peace is therefore only another way of insisting on the undifferentiated character of the interests constitutive of world order and American security.

If interests, like peace, are indivisible, it follows that there is little merit in the distinction between intrinsic and symbolic interests. Indeed, that distinction must prove positively dangerous, insofar as it appears to suggest that symbolic interests are—or may be—less important. The distinction implies that interests may be distinguished and graded (though it clearly does not imply that symbolic interests are thereby unimportant or less important than intrinsic ones). For this reason alone the distinction must be resisted. More to the point, however, it must be resisted for the reason that in the rivalry with communist powers, a rivalry that is both hegemonial and ideological, not only does every interest have a symbolic value, it is precisely the symbolic value that is of crucial significance. The failure of critics to see this stems presumably from their inability to see the rivalry as well as American security in other than conventional power terms. Instead, each confrontation must be looked upon as a test of one's overall resolve, as a symbol of the whole and as related to the underlying conflict over how the world is to be organized. To distinguish interests in terms of their intrinsic and symbolic value can only serve to erode resolve and must thereby jeopardize the order, and security, which rest upon this resolve.

Given the above view, it follows that there are no conflicts in which an unfavorable disparity of wills may arise to threaten the successful implementation of American foreign policy. It is, of course, a commonplace that most conflicts—most, not all—do involve a disparity of wills as between the participants. It is equally a commonplace that this disparity will favor, all other things being equal, the side that has the greater interest in the outcome of the conflict.[14] Even if all other things are not equal, even if there is a considerable disparity of material power between the participants, a sufficient disparity of wills favorable to the weaker party may compensate—through a greater readiness to sacrifice—for this inferiority. Given the outlook toward interests that has informed American foreign policy, however, the possibility of a disparity of wills unfavorable to this nation is very nearly ruled out, and particularly in conflicts with communist states. If every interest of policy is indissolubly bound to every

[14] This is so, of course, for the reason that will ordinarily reflects interest. A disparity of wills, therefore, ordinarily reflects a disparity of interests. We need not take up the problem here of how and why disparities of interest arise. It is sufficient to observe that they do characterize most conflicts and that their determination involves neither arcane procedures nor complex theoretical models.

other, if each confrontation is seen as a test of our over-all resolve, if any conflict in which we engage must determine the prospects for world order and American security, an unfavorable disparity of wills is precluded almost as a matter of principle.

This near refusal to take seriously the possibility of a disparity of wills is also the result of what we have earlier referred to as the traditional American interpretation of conflict in which war is not only an evil but an unnecessary evil. When nations resort to force, they choose a course of action they might readily have avoided. Aggression, therefore, is the result of deliberate evil wedded to accident, the accident of miscalculation. This being so, peace is above all dependent upon insuring—through a policy of deterrence—that would-be aggressors are never given the opportunity to miscalculate, a task that should not prove too formidable precisely because would-be aggressors have no real need to resort to force. The ends of aggression, then, can rarely, if indeed ever, appear so important to an aggressor as to justify the risks that attempting to obtain them by force might impose. Experience may confound dogma, however, and afford examples of very determined "aggressors." In these instances, if our will is to prove triumphant, it can do so only if each test of wills, and therefore each interest, is identified with our vital interests as a nation and with our over-all purposes in the world. Nothing could be more fatal to the success of a deterrent strategy—whether nuclear or otherwise—than attempting to isolate the immediate issue in dispute, thereby separating it from the larger issues to which it is related or for which it must serve as an essential symbol.

The persistence of the conviction of an ever-triumphant will, a will that is ever triumphant because of the interests and purposes it reflects, shows its independence of strategic theories. In an earlier period of the cold war it did not seem unreasonable to link this conviction to a strategy of nuclear deterrence whose active implementation carried very great—and to many, radically exorbitant—risks. A strategy of nuclear deterrence carrying such risks, it was urged, almost compelled this conviction. If the will to deter aggression depends on the conviction that the interests served by nuclear deterrence justify the risks incurred in invoking this strategy, the interests must of necessity appear very great indeed. Without this conviction a strategy of nuclear deterrence is readily deprived both of its political and moral justification. So the argument of critics ran. Yet it is ironic that although the deterrent strategy of an earlier period is now discredited, its essential logic has not been abandoned by the strategy that succeeded. In the one major application we have had to date of escalation theory, it is apparent that the success of what is initially a very limited application of force is made ultimately dependent on the same conviction that earlier informed a strategy of nuclear deterrence. The difference is that whereas in the latter theory this conviction of an ever-triumphant will is explicit, in the former theory it is no more than implicit and, as it were, only becomes explicit in the course of a war that steadily mounts in its intensity.

The rationale for the American commitment in Vietnam evidently affords a striking—one is tempted to say a perfect—illustration of the themes developed in preceding pages. In its essential form that rationale has no novel elements distinguishing it from the views set forth by earlier administrations. Although there are variations in emphasis, what is significant is the element of continuity. "Why are we in Vietnam?" For those who have grasped the deeper meaning of American foreign policy over the past generation this familiar question of administration spokesmen can be no more than rhetorical. The problem of Vietnam is a problem of how the peace of the world is to be organized and maintained. Is that order, and the peace it implies, to be one of consent or one of coercion, one which safeguards the right of self-determination or one which destroys this right, one which provides an environment favorable to the growth of free institutions or one which encourages the spread of arbitrary and irresponsible power? This is the ultimate issue that two administrations have found at stake in Vietnam. It is an issue that is seen to transcend Vietnam and Southeast Asia, however important the immediate interest in preserving the integrity of the region. It is presumably the same fundamental issue that the Truman Doctrine responded to a generation ago in calling for, and in initiating, the historic transformation in American foreign policy.

It is, of course, the equation of world order and American security upon which the administration's defense of Vietnam must ultimately stand or fall. That equation, it is important to insist, does not depend, and has never been made to depend, upon the denial of circumstances apparent even to the casual observer. To this extent, critics who labor the differences between Europe and Asia, and the consequent difficulties attending containment of communism in Asia, are pushing at open doors, since no one denies the differences. (It is another matter to assert that these differences not only render difficult but in fact must preclude the success of a policy of containment, military and otherwise, in Asia. But this claim is by no means apparent.) The same must be said of the insistence with which critics of Vietnam have called attention to the fact that communism is no longer monolithic. However slow American policy-makers may have been to appreciate the breakdown of communist unity, the fact of this breakdown has not been in dispute during the controversy over Vietnam. What has been very much in dispute is the significance of this breakdown, particularly in the context of Vietnam. For most of the critics the significance of communist disunity is that, even at this late date, an American defeat in Vietnam would probably have no more than local effects. For supporters of the war, the fact of communist disunity cannot with safety be relied upon to limit the effects of a communist victory, presumably because the effects of a communist victory in South Vietnam would be limited neither by the independence of Hanoi nor by the breach between Moscow and Peking. A victory for Hanoi must and will be seen as a victory of Hanoi's major allies and supporters. That the allies of North Vietnam are antagonistic to each other, that they differ radically even over the desired outcome in Vietnam, can only mean that the challenge to the present structure of world order consequent upon an American defeat in Vietnam would not be centrally directed. It cannot mean that there would be no challenge. Nor can it be taken to mean that this challenge would be confined to Southeast Asia or even to Asia as a whole.

After three years of large-scale American involvement in Vietnam we still do not know whether the détente with the Soviet Union following the Cuban missile crisis has been hindered or helped by our actions in Vietnam. But even if it is assumed that Vietnam has had an adverse affect upon Soviet-American relations, it does not follow that an American defeat would improve those relations. On the contrary, if the past is at all relevant for the future, the contrary conclusion must be drawn. Defeat in Vietnam, let alone the abandonment of Vietnam, might not thereby undo the effects of the cold war, but it would be rash to assert that a defeat would not place those effects in question. Defeat in Vietnam might not present the Soviets with an irresistible temptation to apply pressure where they have not done so in the years following the Cuban missile crisis, but it would be rash to assert that a defeat would not at least encourage this temptation, with the result of bringing about situations in which there is a danger that nuclear weapons might be threatened or used.

In sum, then, the central contention has been and remains that failure in Vietnam will place in jeopardy the efforts of twenty years. Even if it were conceded that the commitment in South Vietnam was unwise in the first place, the relevant consideration, it is argued, is that the commitment was made. Having been made, there remains no alternative but to honor it. The failure to do so, as administration spokesmen never tire of pointing out, is to undermine faith in the American commitment elsewhere; it is to undermine faith even in the commitment made to those who may express doubt and dissatisfaction over American actions in Vietnam. The integrity of the American commitment is therefore at the heart of the problem in Vietnam. Fail on that commitment and all else will once again be placed in doubt. Vindicate that commitment and not only will the so-far desirable outcome of the cold war be further consolidated, but a substantial step will have been taken toward tempering and moderating a revolution in Asia that as yet refuses to adjust in conduct and aspiration to the style and norms of a more conventional statecraft.

What are we to say of this argument? Can it be said that to the degree it is true it is a self-fulfilling truth? In part, it is of course just that. To justify an ever-expanding commitment in Vietnam the commitment had to be seen as vindicating ever expanding, and vital, interests. To dissuade the adversary from matching that commitment, to persuade him of our seriousness and determination, it was necessary first to persuade ourselves that Vietnam represented vital American interests. For only in this manner could we persuade ourselves, and presumably the adversary as well, that our interests in the outcome of the war were such as to create a disparity of wills favorable to us. Moreover, that favorable disparity of wills, when taken together with our vast material superiority, would not only deter the adversary from continuing the conflict beyond a certain point, it would also deter the adversary's allies from supporting him beyond a certain point. But this by now familiar criticism may be, and frequently has been, pushed too far. The significance Vietnam has come to represent, and came to represent by 1965, was not simply a matter of our creation. In part, that significance was the inevitable outcome of the hegemonial conflict with both the Soviet Union and

China, a conflict in which each disputed interest is seen on both or all sides as a symbol of the whole conflict, and in which each confrontation, whether direct or indirect, is looked upon by adversaries as a test case. If Vietnam has been regarded as a test case for communist wars of national liberation, however misplaced it may be to so regard it, no useful purpose is served by insisting that this alleged test case was little more than the invention of American policy-makers.

It is, in fact, impossible to deny a certain plausibility to the administration's rationale for the commitment in Vietnam, if only because projections of security ultimately rest on assumptions which have no satisfactory means of validation before the disputed result (after which validation may be superfluous). The lessons of history may be plausibly invoked in support of varying, if not contradictory, assumptions. Then, too, in a period when the bases of security have been largely transformed, it may be argued that the lessons of the past, quite apart from their ambiguity, can have no more than a limited relevance for the present. Indeed, despite the constant emphasis of administration spokesmen in defending Vietnam by invoking the lessons of history, it is not so much the lessons of the past that they have invoked but what are assumed to be the lessons of the present, lessons that are held to result from the transformed nature of the security problem. Finally, and perhaps most significantly, the plausibility of the administration's position results, ironically enough, precisely from an argument that cannot be openly made, that is, the argument that national security may come to depend upon imperial security, that the protection of conventional, yet vital, national interests may come to depend upon the protection of imperial interests. This argument has formed the staple of the defense of empire through the ages. That there are scarcely any limits to what it can justify and has justified, once it is accepted, cannot be taken to prove that it is without substance, for it does possess a measure of truth despite its potentiality for abuse. To have achieved an imperial position may have been unwise, if at all avoidable. To hold on to that position may involve danger and certainly sacrifice. Even so, to surrender that position to hostile forces may involve no less, and more likely far greater, danger.[15] As applied to America today, this is not the argument that the world must have order and that such order will be imposed by the powerful. Nor is it the argument that the world must have order and order presupposes, even necessitates, a guarantor. (The latter argument is, after all, little more than a euphemistic way of stating the former argument, given the nature of international society.) Instead, it is the argument that the world must have order—even more, a certain kind of order—because America's security as a nation is inseparable from the preservation of a certain kind of order. Once again, then, we have come back to the larger issue from which we began.

[15] The powerful, this argument runs, are in reality the prisoners of their power, just as the rich are in reality the prisoners of their riches. It is an argument compounded of truth and falsehood, despite the fact that the terrible burdens of power have seldom tempted the powerful voluntarily to yield their power, just as the burdens of riches have seldom tempted the rich to disavow their riches.

III. THE CRITICISM OF AMERICAN FOREIGN POLICY

It is easier to summarize the affirmation of American foreign policy than the criticism of it. It is not surprising that this should be so. In the nature of things the affirmation of foreign policy will have a substantial degree of organization, unity, and direction. Critics, on the other hand, may have no other bond than their criticism. Thus as between the critics comprising the new left and many critics who until recently formed a part of the foreign policy consensus there may be little that is common apart from opposition to Vietnam (and even that bond must be qualified in terms of the reasons for and depths of the opposition to the war). To the degree that this opposition goes beyond Vietnam and deals with Asian containment policy generally, it has proceeded from different assumptions and reached equally different policy conclusions. Again apart from the war in Vietnam, there may be little common ground between the new left and those in the peace movement whose opposition to the war stems largely from a pacifist commitment. Here, as elsewhere, alliances formed to oppose administration policy in Vietnam have rested on a narrow and insubstantial base. Finally, there remain significant differences among the "moderate" and "realist" critics who have been in the mainstream of the postwar American approach to international politics. For the mainstream is still broad and holds within it quite different fish.

Is there at least a general issue around which criticism has centered, an issue that by virtue of its salience gives a certain unity to the criticism? Clearly there is: it is the issue of intervention. Although it does not comprise the whole of the criticism directed against American foreign policy, it is unmistakably at the center of that criticism. If the present debate would not have arisen in the absence of Vietnam, the general issue Vietnam evidently must raise is the issue of intervention. The point is unexceptionable. At the same time, the utility of using the issue of intervention—the core of which remains, as always, the problem of force—as a means for giving unity and coherence to an otherwise apparent variety of criticism may prove limited, if only because intervention is *the* issue of foreign policy, the issue about which most other issues ultimately turn. To say that the focus of the present debate is the issue of intervention may prove tantamount to saying, in view of the generality of this issue, that the debate has no clear focus.

Despite the generality of the issue of intervention, it would still make sense to structure the present debate, hence the criticism of American foreign policy, primarily around it if most of the critics shared roughly the same anti-interventionist outlook. There have been earlier periods in American history when great debates over foreign policy could be characterized, without much distortion, as between interventionists and anti-interventionists, as debates over the issue of intervention pure and simple. But the time has long passed when debate could, and did, mainly center on whether the United States has interests outside this hemisphere requiring intervention. In this literal sense, the debate has not been one between interventionists and noninterventionists. On the contrary, it is more accurately characterized as one between interventionists and interventionists, for the majority of the more articulate and influential critics are not anti-interventionist in principle. Indeed, until very recently most of them generally supported a policy which can scarcely be termed anti-interventionist. There is no reason or justification for equating their defection over Vietnam with anti-interventionism per se when some of them first supported the war, when others did not oppose the war in its earlier stages, and when still others, although opposing the Vietnamese intervention throughout, have advocated intervention in Asia, if necessary, to meet and contain direct Chinese military expansion. Given this checkered record, it is not even accurate to describe the anti-interventionism of most critics as applicable, without qualification, to internal or civil conflicts. For it is not that they oppose intervening in any and all civil conflicts—at least, not yet—but rather the kind of conflict we have encountered in Vietnam.

Nor is this all. Even among those critics who may be termed qualified anti-interventionists, though not anti-interventionist in principle, there are marked disparities in outlook and interest. A substantial number are qualified anti-interventionists not because they disagree over the interests and purposes of American foreign policy but because they are persuaded that, in many situations, and particularly in predominantly revolutionary conflicts, intervention is an ineffective and even counterproductive means for realizing these interests and purposes. They are the "critics of means," not of the ends or broad interests of policy. They largely share the expansive views of America's world role and security that have marked American policy through four administrations. A relatively small number do not share this expansive view of America's world role, and have a much more restricted view of the nation's vital, and indeed legitimate, interests. They may find most interventions ineffective and even counterproductive, they may find the penchant for intervention as leading to the overextension of American power, but these considerations do not form the root cause of their qualified anti-interventionism. Despite a critique that may concentrate on the means of policy, and often unduly so, the essence of their disagreement is over the interests, purposes, and outlook of a policy that has led to ill-advised and unwanted interventions. This is why for the latter group the criticism of American foreign policy is almost invariably informed by a wide-ranging critique of the nation's diplomatic "style" and the errors and dilemmas to which this style has presumably led. At the root of the American crisis in foreign policy, then, is a failure of political intelligence, an incapacity to see the world for what it is rather than what we would like it to be, and, consequently, an unwillingness to accept and adjust to the "real" world with its never-ending conflict and strife. A mindless, if not quite evil, interventionism is thus held to be the almost inevitable consequence of this crusading style marked by its unlimited aspirations and its inability to make those distinctions necessary for a rational and effective foreign policy, a style for which the term "globalism" has come to stand as the common synonym.

Is it possible and preferable to substitute geography for intervention as a general issue of criticism? Is the disaffection with American policy roughly proportionate to the degree to which the focus of policy has shifted from Europe (and, to a lesser extent, from Latin America as well) to Asia? Clearly, there is much to be said for this view. The foreign policy consensus of the past generation had a geographical center of gravity in Europe. That consensus reflected the unique importance of Europe to America as well as the initial agreement on the nature of the threat to Europe and the policy of countering it. In contrast, the American interest in Asia has always been less clear and the nature of the threat subject to constant disagreement. Consequently, at no time in the entire postwar period has there been a measure of agreement over policy in Asia that equalled the agreement obtained in the early years of the cold war over Europe. To the extent that there has been a kind of consensus over Asian policy, it has been, as noted, a negative consensus. Even so, the utility of structuring criticism principally around geography also has limits. The consensus over European policy began to wane by the middle nineteen-fifties. Since then that policy has been an object of contention as much as of consensus. Despite the continued unique importance of Europe, it may therefore be argued that the unusual measure of early agreement on European policy is to be attributed to an equally unusual set of circumstances, which probably cannot be recreated today even in Europe. If European policy does not incur the widespread and intense criticism of Asian policy, it may in part be because European policy no longer seems very consequential, either in the initiatives it appears to compel (or, for that matter, afford) or in the price it entails.

Then, too, the distinctive nature of the war in Vietnam must itself qualify the thesis that present disaffection with American policy is the result of its predominantly Asian focus. Even if it is true that disagreement has marked America's Asian policy throughout, and that this policy has never enjoyed more than a negative consensus, it is also true that this negative consensus was put to a test in circumstances which could scarcely have been less fortunate. Unless American policy in Vietnam is to be equated with America's Asian policy as a whole, opposition to the war in Vietnam ought not to be equated with opposition to the foundations on which this broader policy presumably rests. In fact, many critics have not made this equation. While opposing the war in Vietnam, they have not opposed the containment of Chinese power. While criticizing what they consider to be a misunderstanding of the nature of the Chinese threat, which is held to be political rather than military in character, they have not opposed a policy appropriate to countering this threat. While discounting the prospect of direct Chinese expansion through conventional military methods, they have not opposed meeting such expansion—should it ever occur—with American military power.[1] What other conclusion can be drawn from this position save that the maintenance of a balance of power in Asia is a vital American interest?

[1] Of course, some critics have consistently opposed this, notably Walter Lippmann. But many clearly have not and others either have obscured the issue or have simply discounted altogether the prospect. And even Lippmann has opposed only the commitment of American forces to a large land war on the mainland of Asia. He has never opposed the use of any and all forms of American military power. Nor could he do so, agreeing as he does with the proposition that the containment of China is a vital American interest.

Finally, note must be taken of the view that the common denominator of criticism is the conviction that domestic policy and needs should have primacy over foreign policy. The coincidence of Vietnam with a severe domestic crisis has evidently strengthened this conviction. Even so, it is argued that the belief in the primacy of domestic policy has never been far below the surface, representing as it does one of our most deeply rooted traditions. The primacy given to foreign policy since World War II must therefore be seen as an aberration of sorts, an aberration that is now giving way to what is, in terms of the nation's experience and belief, the normal condition. It is within the general context of the reassertion of the primacy of domestic policy, then, that we may understand the otherwise diverse strands of contemporary criticism as well as the renaissance today of traditional themes: that the alleged necessities of foreign policy, certainly of an imperial policy, must ultimately erode domestic institutions and liberties; that the sacrifices demanded in the name of reason of state must be made at the price of needed domestic reform; and that the American purpose can instead best be realized in the world by the force of the example we set at home.

This view must not be taken literally. There is no significant group of critics who have argued for the primacy of domestic over foreign policy regardless of circumstance and interest. Even if most critics, in George Kennan's telling division, wish to conduct foreign policy in order to live rather than live in order to conduct foreign policy, this does not mean that domestic policy is given primacy over foreign policy. Instead, it means that the physical security of the nation and the integrity of its institutions form the central purpose and justification of foreign policy and that the expenditure of treasure and blood for purposes other than these must always be questioned.

It is in this modified sense that the above view is to be taken. And in this sense there is no question but that it points to a general characteristic of contemporary dissent. It is true that this form of dissent has never been absent in the course of the cold war. Until quite recently, however, it was rather muted. It is only in recent years that the insistance on redressing what is considered to be a dangerous imbalance between foreign and domestic policy has gained widespread expression and acceptance. Thus the assertion that we are overcommitted in foreign policy has almost become a password of critics, accepted for the most part without further question, despite the fact that we are no more committed today, relative to our material resources, than we have been for twenty years. The argument that we are now overcommitted is clearly unpersuasive if made in material terms and in terms relative to past commitments and resources. It may prove quite persuasive, however, if made in terms of an altered order of priorities that results either from what is believed to be a recession of the security threat, or from fatigue—and some disillusion—with foreign involvements, or from a sudden appreciation of the importance and urgency of domestic reforms (or, as appears to be the case, from a combination of these factors).

However significant this renewed emphasis on the primacy of domestic policy, it is as difficult to structure the criticism of American foreign policy around this theme as around the issue of intervention. In both cases, the issues are very general; what is represented as a focus of debate, on examination seems to indicate that the debate has no clear focus. The insistence that there is at present an unwanted, and even dangerous, imbalance between foreign and domestic policy does clearly indicate a certain tendency, a certain orientation. But that may be all, given the disparity of view it otherwise comprises. Moreover, this disparity of view need not be measurably narrowed by common adherence to the position that the physical security of the nation and the integrity of its institutions form the central purpose and justification of foreign policy. Without further qualification, that position is far less astringent than many critics appear to believe. There is no reason why it should not elicit the agreement of those who affirm American foreign policy, as, indeed, it does. It leaves in abeyance not only the meaning of security today but, by so doing, the relation of security to purpose.

The issues considered in the preceding pages are neither individually sufficient nor mutually exclusive, and recognizing this, the most forceful critics have combined them and added another ingredient, the historical perspective. We may best understand where we are today, this criticism runs, by understanding where we were a generation ago, and where we have been in the intervening period. We may best understand the present inadequacies of American foreign policy by understanding the conditions and policies from which present policy has grown. The issues of intervention, anticommunism, Europe versus Asia, etc., are thus considered in their historical context. The historical criticism is also varied, and any attempt to summarize its expression is partly artificial. Apart from a tiresome inventory of views, however, there is no escape from this.

For critics of American foreign policy the history of the nation's diplomacy since the immediate post-World-War-II years is largely a history of decline. It is the history of a diplomacy that has turned almost full circle from clarity of concept, at least at the level of practical action, to obscurantism, and from modesty of action, to what can only be termed a virtual compulsion for the disproportionate act. It is the history of a diplomacy that was once seen by most of the world as the instrument of a progressive and liberating nation and is now seen as the instrument of an increasingly repressive and "counter-revolutionary" imperial America. It is the history of a diplomacy that once responded to the true interests of America but no longer does. Although the world has changed, and changed profoundly, in the course of the past generation, we have not changed with it. "If there is a single indictment of the multiple and self-contradictory forms that American globalism takes," two critics assert, "it is simply that its arguments and rationales are out of date."[2] "To characterize American foreign policy in one sentence," another declares, "one could say that it has lived during the last decade or so on the intellectual capital which was accumulated in the famous fifteen weeks of the spring of 1947 . . . and that this capital has now

[2] Edmund Stillmann and William Pfaff, *Power and Impotence: The Failure of America's Foreign Policy* (1966), p. 62.

been nearly exhausted."[3] Moreover, what might still prove valid today in earlier policy has long since been eroded, whether through misunderstanding or deliberate rejection. Reviewing the history of American diplomacy since 1947, the author of the first crucial statement of postwar American containment policy concludes: "One by one, its essential elements were abandoned."[4] Thus a policy initially designed to restore and maintain a balance of power has been replaced by a policy that scorns so modest an objective. A policy once reasonably tolerant of revolutionary change has been succeeded by a policy intolerant of such change because of an obsessive fear of communism and an equally obsessive identification of revolutionary change with communism. Finally, a former reluctance to employ force save on behalf of narrowly construed vital interests has given way to the assertion of a right, and, indeed, an obligation, to take whatever measures deemed necessary to prevent violent changes in the status quo.[5]

[3] Hans J. Morgenthau, "A New Foreign Policy for the United States: Basic Issues," *Bulletin of the Atomic Scientists* (January 1967), p. 7.

[4] George F. Kennan, "The Quest for Concept," *Harvard Today* (September 1967), p. 16.

[5] It is the assertion of this right, and obligation, that is held up as perhaps the essential feature marking America's policy as imperial, and even "imperialistic." Thus one critic writes: "In assuming that we have an obligation to smother violent changes in the status quo by discontented groups within various countries, we are arrogating to ourselves the responsibility for being an international police power. We are doing so without anyone's consent and from no other motive than that we believe that our vision of a proper political order is valid for nations everywhere. This, whether we recognize it or not, is imperialism. . . ." Ronald Steel, *Pax Americana* (1967), p. 325.

The revisionists apart,[6] then, the early years of containment are seen by most critics as the heroic period of American foreign policy. It is during this period of the late forties that American policy registered its greatest successes, and, to the more austere critics, its only real successes. The geographical focus of that policy was Europe; the object was to restore a balance of power destroyed by the war. The Marshall Plan and its military counterpart, the North Atlantic Alliance, were the principal measures of the grand design for restoring western Europe, economically, politically, and socially, thereby assuring that these nations would not fall under Soviet control as a result either of internal political change or of Soviet military attack. It is true that even in this early period, as today, the nature of the threat was subject to dispute. To some it appeared, and time has not altered their earlier judgment, that the threat posed by the Soviet Union to western Europe was primarily political rather than military, that the danger was one of communist revolution and subversion rather than of a Soviet military attack. In this view the North Atlantic Alliance was at best an unnecessary measure and at

[6] This essay does not examine the growing revisionist literature on the Cold War. Rather than to justify this omission by dismissing the arguments of the revisionists it seems better to remain silent on the merits of their arguments. It is not unfair to say, however, that few revisionists number among the currently influential critics of American foreign policy. This is true even of a William A. Williams (*The Tragedy of American Diplomacy*), whose influence in shaping the views of the cold war held by the younger generation will almost surely prove very considerable. Indeed, once torn from their Marxist setting, a number of the views Williams expressed a decade ago (e.g., "an open door for revolution") have now become accepted currency among the more respectable critics.

worst a harmful one, in that by providing the formal basis for an American military presence in western Europe it increased the prospect of a prolonged division of Europe. But this view neglects the insecurity experienced as a result of the nearby presence of the Red Army, a presence that lent indirect support and encouragement to communist minorities in western Europe while hindering the efforts of governments to restore economic and political stability. For most of today's critics the threat to western Europe in the late nineteen-forties was both political and military; hence a military guarantee formed part of the necessary response. (The parallel between the above view and the argument of many Asian containment critics today is clear. Where the parallel ends is, of course, in the assumptions made then and now about the effects of internal political changes resulting in the seizure of power by communist minorities. Whereas in the earlier period such change was seen to add to Soviet power and prestige, today the seizure of power by communist groups is not seen as necessarily adding to Soviet or Chinese power and prestige in view of the nationalist propensities of communist regimes.)

If the early containment policy was modest and limited both in its geographical scope and in its objectives, the success of that policy is nevertheless seen to have been made possible only by a combination of uniquely favorable circumstances, the most important being the unparalleled power and prestige with which America emerged from the war. The atomic monopoly enjoyed in those years was only the most vivid manifestation of what was eventually to prove an artificially favorable position. Almost equally artificial in its very simplicity was the nature of the contest in which America was progressively engaged. On one of those rare occasions in history two great powers confronted each other alone and unhindered by third parties, for the rest of a prostrate world could form no more than the passive object of the confrontation. Moreover, given the stark simplicity of this confrontation, the issue that later was to plague American policy makers remained for the time largely irrelevant. Whether containment was to be directed against Soviet power or communism itself, or both, was not an issue of practical importance so long as communism remained monolithic Soviet communism acting as an agent of Russian imperialism. Clearly, it did not appear as an important issue in western Europe, the control of which formed the principal occasion for, and stake of, the conflict. Finally, and perhaps most importantly, were the favorable, indeed, the almost perfect, conditions for carrying out a policy of containment. In every sense —culturally, politically, and militarily—western Europe was accessible and responsive to America and to American power.

It is the common theme of critics that our later failures were born in part from our early success. For this success not only appeared to confirm the general outlook expressed by the Truman Doctrine, it also gave rise to the conviction that containment in Europe was a model to be applied elsewhere. Whereas the early policy of containment was Eurocentric, directed primarily against the expansion of Soviet power, and designed to restore a balance of power, the Truman Doctrine was unlimited in geographic scope, directed against communism itself, and proclaimed the objective of assisting all peoples to work out their destinies in freedom. This disparity between policy and doctrine did not at first seem very significant in view of the triumph of policy. For whatever the verbal excesses of the Truman Doctrine, in the early policy of containment these excesses were not translated into practice. Yet it was the very triumph of early policy that helped to pave the way for the gradual triumph of doctrine and, consequently, for the translation of doctrine into policy. The gradual universalization of the Truman Doctrine in the realm of policy was therefore attended by the attempt to apply outside Europe the same successful combination of methods—economic aid and military alliance. In the absence of conditions favorable to the effective application of these methods, a policy which succeeded in Europe was bound to fail elsewhere.

In the historiography of the critics there is no consensus over the point in time that the decline began. To a few it began even before Korea with the decision to establish NATO. To others it began with Korea and the forces set in motion by Korea. To still others it began only with the administration that succeeded the Truman administration. This disagreement is more than academic for it reflects a continuing disagreement over the significance initially attached to the Truman Doctrine and the relationship between it and the early policy of containment. For those who trace the decline from Korea, or, better yet, from the end of the Truman administration, the marked contrast between the "realism" of early containment policy and the "sentimentalism" of the Truman Doctrine indicates that the excesses of the latter may be explained by the exigencies of satisfying, yet arousing, public opinion. Thus one historian of the cold war writes of the commitment in the Truman Doctrine to a universal crusade for freedom and justice: "I suspect that the significance of this sentence, thrown in by public-relations specialists, was not fully appreciated at the time."[7] But this view is not supported by the most authoritative account of the origins of the Truman Doctrine (Joseph M. Jones, *The Fifteen Weeks* [1955]), which makes clear that the universal character of the Doctrine was appreciated at the time. Nor do the limits of early containment policy prove that for those in the Truman administration the Truman Doctrine was mere rhetoric, though rhetoric taken seriously by succeeding administrations. It only "proves" what needs no proof: that containment was initially limited to the area of unique interest to America. That the Truman administration did not simultaneously apply containment to Asia, particularly by entangling itself in the Chinese civil war, scarcely proves that it did not take the Truman Doctrine seriously. In the circumstances of 1946–48 it was difficult enough to obtain broad public support for the new policy in Europe, where, after all, American security was most immediately and clearly threatened. Moreover, the subsequent extension of containment to Asia was undertaken by the Truman administration in the course of the Korean War. Succeeding administrations consolidated this extension, but they clearly did not initiate it.

These differences apart, the beginning of our time of troubles may be dated as early as the period of

[7] Louis J. Halle, *The Cold War as History* (1967), p. 121.

the Korean War. All great conflicts gather a momentum of their own which persists and grows after the causes that initially provoked the conflict have, if not disappeared, at least abated. The cold war conformed to this experience. Not only did it arouse fears that could not be readily quieted once the threats that provoked them had begun to recede, its inner dynamic provoked new fears. But if this general tendency of great conflicts appears inevitable, the degree to which it is realized in any given conflict depends upon contingent events. The Korean conflict, frustrating and disappointing in outcome as it appeared to most of the nation, hardened attitudes and led to an increasingly ideological view of the cold war. The chief adversary became communism itself rather than Soviet, and later Chinese, imperialism. And although the central significance of Korea must be found in Europe, the effect of Korea was to generalize the cold war by extending containment to Asia, with all the momentous consequences of that extension. Alliances were subsequently formed with governments that all too often had little, if any, popular support. Given the weaknesses of these governments, the outcome of the new alliance relationships was predictable. Whereas it was never really possible to establish imperial relations with the European states, it has proved difficult to establish anything but imperial relations with most Asian states.

Even in Europe the Korean conflict is frequently held to have had a baneful effect, not so much for the impetus it gave to the military buildup of NATO—though, in retrospect, many consider that buildup to have been unnecessary and productive of added tension—as for the pressure it generated to incorporate Western Germany in the Atlantic Alliance. This incorporation of Western Germany, and its subsequent rearmament, whatever the immediate effects on European security, consolidated the division of Europe and rendered negligible for the foreseeable future the prospects of a negotiated settlement.[8]

These effects of the Korean conflict —an increasingly ideological view of the cold war, the extension of containment to Asia, the freezing of European policy—occurred when the postwar configuration was already beginning to show signs of change. By the middle nineteen-fifties the revival of western Europe and the recession of the threat that had stimulated the American intervention were becoming accomplished facts. In the communist world, although the emerging schism between the two major communist states was not yet apparent, the attempt by the eastern European states to assert a measure of independence from Soviet control was all too apparent. Elsewhere, the colonial revolution was reaching its culmination, and the new states were fast becoming one of the principal stakes of Soviet-American competition.

It was in these circumstances that American policy began to falter and to lose sight of its initial objectives. In the view of a number of critics American policy began to falter and lose sight of its original objectives precisely because the focus of policy was transferred to the underdeveloped states of the

[8] The emphasis with which the latter point is made will depend, of course, upon the estimate made of the prospects of a negotiated settlement. Critics have varied, and considerably so, in their estimates of these prospects even before the incorporation of Germany into the Western Alliance.

southern hemisphere. With the change of focus, it is contended, a political struggle fought for real stakes, for vital national interests, was transformed into a moral combat involving illusory, that is, ideological, stakes. In part, this view is based on the conviction, or estimate, of the relative unimportance of the underdeveloped states in the present and future balance of world power. In part, however, it is based on what is felt to be the uncertainty and even the intangibility of the stakes. Whereas Europe conformed to the traditional power struggles, the underdeveloped states presumably do not. Whereas the stake in Europe was the control of territory, the stake in the underdeveloped states is the alliance, or allegiance, of normally unstable and unreliable governments. To other critics American policy began to falter simply because we had begun to manifest that resistance to change that has since become the dominant feature of our policy. Although the simple postwar bipolar configuration was yielding to a more complex international system, we persisted in a view of the world that had been formed a decade earlier. Although the force of nationalism was already challenging the specter of a monolithic communist world, we insisted upon identifying communism everywhere with the extension of Soviet, or Sino-Soviet, power. Through an increasingly ideological interpretation of the cold war and the extension of it to Asia and Africa, a policy originally centered in Europe was transformed into a policy that had no geographical limitations and consequently drew no geographical distinctions because its principal object had become nothing less than preservation of the status quo wherever it was seemingly threatened by communism.

101

The day of reckoning was put off, however, in part because of the innate caution of the Eisenhower administration and in much larger part because of the circumstances of the Cuban missile crisis, the last great crisis in Soviet-American relations. It must be recalled that from late 1958 to late 1962 the Soviets mounted their most ambitious challenge to the American position. The years in question begin with Khrushchev's declaration that the issue of Berlin had become intolerable and had to be resolved in accordance with Soviet demands; they end with the abortive Soviet move to place strategic weapons in Cuba, thereby altering the strategic balance and presenting a direct challenge to America's hegemonial position in the western hemisphere. These same years are also marked by declining American confidence that in the competition with the communist world time was necessarily on the western side, that events were necessarily moving in a manner favorable to American interests. At the level of strategic military power, it was widely believed—at least until mid 1961—that a gap was developing to the Soviet's advantage as a result of what was assumed to be a Soviet lead in missile development. More generally, the expectancy, particularly strong in the early period of the Kennedy administration, that the Soviets and Chinese would be the principal benefactors in the competition for the allegiance of the new states contributed to the general pessimism. Finally, although the difficulties besetting the Western Alliance were apparent to all, the far more portentous developments taking place in the communist bloc were not so apparent.

In these circumstances, the difficulties that had increasingly beset American policy in the nineteen-fifties receded in importance, or, at least, from view. Instead, there occurred a kind of return to the earlier atmosphere, and even the conditions, of the cold war. It is only with the passing of the Cuban crisis that difficulties long in the making reappeared, and with a vengeance. For if America emerged from the crisis with an exaggerated sense of its power relative to others, and what that power could accomplish, it did not emerge with a heightened sense of security. Whereas before the principal source of insecurity had been the threat of Soviet expansion, now it was the threat of Chinese expansion and, even more, of communist expansion generally. Whereas in the early period of containment American security had been primarily identified with the restoration and maintenance of a favorable balance of power, now it was identified with the maintenance of an order—in effect, the status quo—that bore little, if any, relation to the balance of power. The constituent principle of that order has been anticommunism, interpreted in practice to require indiscriminate American opposition to revolutionary violence. Thus the recession of the real danger that once led to America's postwar intervention in Europe has been replaced by a multitude of dangers, many of which are imaginary, that have prompted a policy of global intervention.

This policy is bound to fail if only for the reason that it reflects a view of the world that is profoundly at odds with reality. Although the world is politically and ideologically pluralistic, American foreign policy proceeds from an assumption—or rather a conviction—that denies this pluralism. Instead, the world of the late nineteen-sixties is interpreted in essentially the same terms as the world of the late nineteen-forties, as a world, in the words of the Truman Doctrine, dominated by a universal conflict between the forces of freedom and unfreedom. If that interpretation was inadequate even a generation ago, at least it bore some resemblance to reality. Today it no longer does so.[9] The results of persisting in this interpretation are already clear. A policy that does not and apparently cannot distinguish between vital and less-than-vital interests is bound to result in the overcommitment of the nation's resources. A policy that insists upon the identification of revolutionary change with communism and the latter with the triumph of the forces of unfreedom is bound to be driven into an increasingly futile counter-revolutionary stance which, if anything, succeeds only in promoting communism. And even when that stance does not prove futile or counterproductive, even when it does not overestimate what intervention can accomplish, it runs the danger of betraying the American purpose both abroad and at home. For in a world that is in many respects more diverse than it has ever been, in a

[9] That we nevertheless persist in this interpretation proves that America is still isolationist in the deeper sense of remaining an "isolated" nation. This quality of isolation, the sense of moral and political separateness, may manifest itself both in a policy of isolation as well as in a policy of intervention. In either case, the root of policy is presumably the same and consists in the inability to recognize and to accept the world for what it is. Instead, the American experience is generalized and American values projected on to the world at large. Thus the messianic hope persists of redeeming history—now through the active employment of American power—by putting an end to the conflicts that have heretofore filled its pages. These themes have been elaborated over the years by such critics as Walter Lippmann, Hans J. Morgenthau, George F. Kennan, and Reinhold Niebuhr. A number of recent critics have laid stress on them in explaining the American diplomatic style.

world that has as many sources of conflict as it has ever had, the American purpose abroad can be directly pursued only through means which, paradoxically, deny that purpose. The denial of that purpose abroad cannot but eventually mean, as the war in Vietnam has shown, its denial at home as well.

Whether explicitly or implicitly, the criticism of American foreign policy raises four major inter-related questions: What are the vital interests of America? What is the nature of the threat to those interests? What can and should be done to preserve those interests? And, finally, what is America's purpose in today's world and how best may that purpose be realized?

It is scarcely surprising that critics should define the primary ends of American foreign policy in general terms that do not set them apart from their opponents. For the critics of American policy, as for those who defend that policy, the great ends of policy must be the nation's physical security, the integrity of its institutions, and the well-being of its citizens. There can be little disagreement, then, over the general proposition set forth in one recent critical study that "a foreign policy is primarily a *defense*, a means by which the social organism defends itself against encroachments and seeks to achieve the international environment within which it can prosper."[10] Nor can there be much disagreement in the nuclear age over the one contingency that would, above all others, jeopardize the great ends of foreign policy. A major nuclear war—probably any nuclear war involving the great pow-

[10] Stillmann and Pfaff, *Power and Impotence*, p. 185.

ers—would threaten America's survival as a nation. Accordingly, its prevention must form the foremost objective of policy. And this must be taken to mean that the prevention of any development that might be expected to significantly increase the danger of nuclear war, for example, nuclear proliferation, constitutes a vital American interest.

The great ends of American foreign policy are not equated by critics simply with the prevention of nuclear war, however important that objective may be. At the very least, these ends are also equated with, or made dependent upon, the preservation of a balance of power in Europe and Asia. Now, as in the past, the maintenance of a favorable balance of power in Europe and Asia is considered a vital American interest. If anything, the more articulate and influential of the critics have gone out of their way to emphasize the continuity of this interest. Thus America is held to have a vital interest in protecting the nations of western Europe against armed aggression (which, in present circumstances, can only mean Soviet aggression), just as she has a vital interest in protecting Japan against armed aggression (which, in present circumstances, can only mean Chinese aggression). Still more generally, America is held to have a vital interest in preventing the industrial and military strength of western Europe and Japan from falling under the control of those who would ally themselves with either the Soviet Union or China. Thus we also have a vital interest in the internal stability and form of government prevailing in western Europe and Japan. These areas are of intrinsic importance because of their power. When added to the strength of a major adversary, the result, it is argued, might well be to turn the balance of world power against us.[11]

Given this definition of America's vital interest in Europe and Asia, *some* kind of policy of containment necessarily follows so long as the Soviet Union and China are deemed to remain even potentially hostile and expansionist powers. To be sure, there is room for disagreement over the kind of containment policy to pursue, particularly in Asia. There is room for disagreement over what is to be contained and the proper means of containment. But if the assumption of potential hostility and expansion is once granted, it is scarcely consistent to affirm the interest and to deny the need for some kind of policy of containment. In fact, with very few exceptions, the leading critics of America's Asian policy have insisted that the containment of China is a vital American interest. They have argued over what is to be contained and the proper means of doing so. They have argued over the prospects of Chinese expansion, particularly military expansion. But, at the very least, they have not questioned the need to contain Chinese military expansion, and

[11] To prevent this possibility from ever materializing, George Kennan declared in the 1966 Vietnam Hearings, "is something that has lain at the heart of my own thinking about these matters ever since 1947." *Hearings before the Senate Committee on Foreign Relations*, 89th Congress, 2d session, February, 1966, p. 424. Kennan added: "If you look around the world and ask yourself where military-industrial strength exists on such a scale that it can produce armed force, and particularly amphibious force, in a degree that can really be troublesome and dangerous to us, you will find that there are really only about five such areas. Our country is one of them; England is another; the Rhine Valley in Western Europe is a third; the Soviet Union is a fourth; and Japan is a fifth."

to do so even when containment and the maintenance of an Asian balance of power are not identical. Thus they have not questioned the need to prevent Chinese military conquest of Southeast Asia
or of India, and this quite apart from balance-of-
power considerations, though they may, and generally do, discount the prospect that would ever
activate this need. Moreover, many critics do not
oppose a policy of containing the political influence
of China in Asia, though they may consider military
containment an ineffective and even a counterproductive means of such a policy.

Has America a vital interest in the western
hemisphere? The critics leave no doubt that it has,
though here again differences arise over the definition of, and the means of protecting, this interest.
For some, the American hemispheric interest permits, and even requires, armed intervention, if
necessary, to prevent the emergence of communist
regimes. Geographical proximity, military security,
and tradition (proprietary rights) sanction in Latin
America what may not be sanctioned, and should
not be undertaken, elsewhere. Others reject the view
that Latin America—or, at the very least, Central
America—forms a sphere of influence of the United
States permitting intervention against communist
regimes. They see American interest requiring intervention only where a communist regime—or, for
that matter, any regime—forms certain kinds of
relationships with either the Soviet Union or China.
In their view, the United States should intervene to
prevent a Latin American state from being transformed into a political and, above all, a military
outpost of a major communist power. A Cuba of
1962 must therefore be prevented, though how this

will always prove possible to prevent, once a state is governed by a communist regime, is generally left unclear. (Even so, we have here what is, in effect, the claim to a sphere of influence, however much that claim may be denied.) For still others, America's vital interest in this hemisphere is vindicated merely by the prevention of foreign (extrahemispheric) aggression. This apparently austere view need not prove to be too restrictive in practice, however, given a sufficient degree of latitude in identifying the elements comprising aggression. Indeed, despite the apparent distinctiveness of these views, they all share one decisive feature. Whatever the definition of America's vital interest in the western hemisphere, each assumes the maintenance of an order of power that insures American hegemony.

The preservation of a favorable balance of power in Europe and Asia and continued hegemony in the western hemisphere do not exhaust, for most critics, America's vital geographical interests. If these are the hard and undisputed core of those interests, they are not considered to form the whole of the interests that may justify the intervention. There are other states whose security and well-being constitute a vital interest to America, even though it is not of a military-strategic character. The rationale of this vital interest, like the list of nations selected, may vary from critic to critic. The rationale can be found in a responsibility to nations which share our culture, institutions, and values; or in the broader responsibility and need to preserve serious and creative societies, societies that have something to contribute to the world, societies the integrity and well-being of which enrich America. In either case, America has a vital interest in preserving a world in which "open" societies may be permitted to remain open, for it is only in such a world that America can itself realize its full potentiality as an open society.

Finally, there are a large number of critics who consider that the *general evolution* of the underdeveloped nations forms a vital American interest. This interest, in their view, clearly does not commit us to global intervention. Still less does it mean that we should seek to universalize American wants and values. It does mean that we have a vital interest in both promoting and defending a pluralistic world. It follows that America is not only committed to resist a course of military conquest in the underdeveloped world, if undertaken by a major communist adversary, but also to resist a strategy of "wars of national liberation" if and when it can be shown that this strategy in a particular instance constitutes a test case. Thus an eminent critic of the war in Vietnam in dismissing the statement that Vietnam is a test case for wars of national liberation and that the outcome of the war will determine the outcome of all such wars nevertheless writes: "If this statement were correct, it would indeed follow that the containment of communism in Vietnam is essential in view of American interests since without it communism would triumph throughout much of the uncommitted world."[12] It is the presumably unique character of the war in Vietnam, then, that in large part explains why opposition to American involvement may not be equated with indifference to the fate of the underdeveloped nations. If what hap-

[12] Morgenthau, "A New Foreign Policy for the United States: Basic Issues," p. 10.

pens in Vietnam has little relevance to the other areas, then however desirable the containment of communism in Vietnam, it is not essential to the interests of the United States.

What conclusions may be drawn from this statement of America's vital interests? It is first of all clear that if these interests are considered in their totality they imply a comprehensive concept of order. They assume a favorable distribution of power. They presuppose that America will continue to occupy a favorable, if not a preponderant, position in the international hierarchy. They restrict the manner in which change may be effected and preclude certain types of change altogether. They afford considerable scope for affinities of institutions and values. Moreover, to assert that these interests are vital to America is, in effect, to assert that America has a vital security interest in maintaining a certain kind of world order, that is, a world order of which these interests make up the component parts. To this extent, at least, it is not only the apologists for American foreign policy who insist on equating America's security as a nation with the preservation of a certain kind of order, for the insistence on making this equation is equally characteristic of the critics.[13]

---

[13] This being so, the folly of Vietnam cannot be established by showing what hardly anyone denies, that Vietnam is of no intrinsic importance. Nor, for that matter, can the folly of Vietnam be established by showing that Vietnam is unique and resembles no other situation in the world (assuming this could be shown). It can be established by showing that the outcome, an adverse outcome, in Vietnam will have little, if any, effect on the structure of world order the critics equate with American security. One important element of that structure, in the view of most critics, is the disposition of nuclear weapons. The proliferation of nuclear weapons would pre-

Nor is this all. Whatever the other differences between these two concepts of order, and hence of security, both refuse to limit security to the physical dimension. In the case of the critics, this refusal is apparent if only in their insistence upon identifying vital interests whose loss would clearly have, in and of themselves, no bearing on America's physical security. Thus no one seriously contends that the continued independence and integrity of an Israel, or an Australia, or even an India is, in and of itself, essential to America's physical security. On the other hand, it is seriously contended that the establishment in this hemisphere of political and military outposts of the Soviet Union would jeopardize American security. And it is accepted almost as self-evident that the preservation of a balance of power in Europe and Asia is a sine qua non of American security. Yet if security is equated with physical security these propositions are no longer self-evident. They are self-evident, or very nearly so, only if one falls back on conventional, prenuclear notions of security. They are persuasive if physical security is still to be calculated primarily in terms of geography, spheres of influence, and industrial concentration. Yet it is precisely the adequacy of conventional balance-of-power calculations in the nuclear age that is at issue.

Why should the loss of once critical areas any longer threaten our physical security? If the one

---

sumably jeopardize that structure and increase the danger of nuclear war. Thus, if an American defeat in Southeast Asia were to lead to the further proliferation of nuclear weapons, it would have to be seen as having a very detrimental effect on the structure of order the critics equate with American security.

contingency that would threaten America's survival as a nation is a nuclear war, the crucial question is what may bring on a nuclear war? Surely the answer to this question is not the additional resources a major hostile power—the Soviet Union or China —might acquire through control over or alliance with states possessed of military-industrial strength. For the addition of these resources could not significantly enhance the prospects of an adversary's survival, let alone of a meaningful victory, in a nuclear war undertaken against the United States. Their addition would enhance, perhaps considerably, the capability to wage limited conflicts in areas of major power contention. Their addition would place in jeopardy, if not end altogether, the possibility of preserving a congenial international environment. Even so, these prospects are not to be equated with America's survival as a nation.

These considerations do not dispose of the question: what may bring on a nuclear war? They do point to the inadequacy of answering this question simply in terms of physical security and in equating physical security with conventional balance-of-power calculations. It is, of course, another matter entirely to argue that although nuclear war is the one contingency that may threaten America's survival as a nation, the risk of nuclear war may nevertheless be run if necessary to preserve other values. The critics no less than the supporters of American foreign policy believe that America's existence has dimensions other than the merely physical dimension, that the nation is something much more than its merely physical attributes. Whether or not America "survives," then, is not an issue that can be considered simply in terms of the attributes that

113

make up the nation's physical person; it must also be considered in terms of a self whose identity requires the preservation of certain values and of the political and social institutions that embody these values. While the loss of areas deemed vital would not thereby render America physically insecure, the result presumably would be to threaten the integrity of our institutions and seriously impair the quality of our domestic life. It is primarily for this reason that the one threat to America's physical survival as a nation has to be risked. The structure of world order the critics equate with American security may have little to do with preserving America's physical survival as a nation; it still has a great deal to do with the question: what may bring on a nuclear war?

Thus the continuity of America's vital interests should not obscure the changes in the significance of these interests. For it is these changes that have given rise to uncertainty and controversy over the conditions, and the very meaning, of American security. Yesterday, interests were considered vital in terms of conventional balance-of-power calculations because, in the first place, their loss could threaten the nation's physical security. Today, the same interests may remain vital, though their loss cannot, as such, threaten our physical security, since that security is no longer dependent on balance-of-power calculations. Because their loss may threaten our security in the broader sense we are willing to risk nuclear war to preserve them. The change thereby effected does not mean that interests may no longer be differentiated and graded in order of importance. It does mean that the task of identifying threats to "vital" interests has become increasingly difficult.

The critical issue in the debate is not so much the issue of what comprises the nation's vital interests as the nature of the treat to them and what can and should be done in defense. The question of interests is, of course, significant. Clearly, there are important differences in the conception of America's vital interests entertained by critics and supporters. The critics have, on the whole, a more restricted conception of the nation's vital interests and for this reason alone, though not only for this reason, a more modest conception of the order necessary to American security. They are, in varying degree, skeptical of the claim—or, at least, the scope given the claim—that the preservation of the institutions of freedom in America is dependent upon the preservation—or eventual realization—of these institutions elsewhere in the world. Even so, these differences may be and frequently are exaggerated, particularly by undue emphasis on the rhetorical excesses of government officials. If these excesses are discounted, if the emphasis is placed on making a world safe for diversity rather than on a world in which American wants and values are universalized, the gap is substantially narrowed. Moreover, the more selective critical view of America's vital interests results from a perception of the threat to American security that differs markedly from that of supporters. What is impressive is the extent of the agreement over interests considered intrinsically vital to America and the nearly complete disagreement over the perception of the threat. Indeed, so fundamental and pervasive is

115

this difference of perception that it almost amounts to two ways of viewing the political world.

The nature of this difference cannot be appreciated, however, by taking at face value the critics' portrayal of American foreign policy and of the consensus on which this policy presumably rests. For that portrayal—or rather caricature—is one of men, and of a policy, insistently blind to the central political realities of the time. The argument that American policy-makers have slept for twenty years and even now refuse to awaken from their dream is surely overdrawn. It is an evident exaggeration to say that American policy reflects an unwillingness to acknowledge that the terms of the cold war have changed, or to insist that the expansion of "communism" anywhere and in any circumstances has the same implications and significance today that it had a generation ago. Nor is it true that American policy reflects a failure to recognize the pluralistic character of contemporary communism and the impact of nationalism on communist movements throughout the world.

If these claims are overdrawn, so also are the critical contentions that the driving force of American foreign policy is little more than a primitively ideological anticommunism and that this obsession explains our intervention in Vietnam. American policy is not dedicated to exorcising communism from the face of the earth. Where communism represents the status quo we are not obsessed with its overthrow, certainly not in Europe. We might wish that the Soviet position in eastern Europe would suffer further erosion and that the eastern European states undergo progressive liberalization. We are prepared to give very restrained encouragement to this evolution. But this is scarcely to be identified with an ideological crusade against communism. Moreover, our attitude and policy toward the Soviet Union is hardly one of ideological crusade, however else it may be described. Indeed, there are some critics who fear that we may now mistakenly move in the opposite direction, so anxious are we to freeze the status quo, and attempt, through a Soviet-American condominium, to invert the terms of the cold war. Even in Asia, American policy cannot be explained simply as an obsessive anticommunism. The containment of China has not been pursued simply because China has a communist government, but because of China's outlook generally and her policy in Asia particularly. It is China's insistence upon changing the Asian status quo, and the methods she has used, that explain American hostility.

This is not to deny that in some sense American foreign policy is anticommunist, since it obviously is. In terms of power realities alone, what else could it be? The principal threat to American interests since World War II has stemmed from communist powers. If there remains a substantial threat today to American interests and to an American concept of world order, however defined, it is principally posed by communist powers. There is room for argument over the intensity of this threat in the past and the extent to which it was the result of communism rather than of more traditional factors. There is room for argument over the nature and scope of the threat that is posed for American interests today by the major communist powers. (Moreover, it is undoubtedly true that the world changes and that our adversaries of today may be

117

our friends of tomorrow.) But until some other, and perhaps even greater, threat appears there is scarcely room for argument over the identity of the one threat, however attenuated it may now be.

There is yet another sense in which American policy is anticommunist, a sense that does border on an ideological anticommunism. It is opposed, in principle, to the emergence of communist governments quite apart from the ways by which they may be established, the foreign policies they might thereafter pursue, the relationships they might establish with the Soviet Union or China, or the effect their emergence alone might have on Soviet or Chinese behavior. It is so opposed because communism is considered an undesirable political and social form for any people, north or south, developed or underdeveloped. But this opposition to communism in principle does not and cannot account for opposition to communist expansion in practice, particularly opposition that takes the form of military intervention. What does in part explain this opposition in practice is the fear that in the underdeveloped world communism may otherwise prove to be the wave of the future. It is the threat, in Robert Heilbroner's words, "that the rise of Communism would signal the end of capitalism as the dominant world order, and would force the acknowledgement that America no longer constituted the model on which the future of world civilization would be mainly based."[14] It is the prospect that the American example and purpose might become irrelevant to much of the world that accounts in part for a

[14] Robert Heilbroner, "Counterrevolutionary America," *Commentary* (April 1967), p. 37.

THE CRITICISM OF AMERICAN FOREIGN POLICY

policy of anticommunism. The prospect of the irrelevance of the American purpose must raise, in turn, the issue of American security. At least it must do so if the proposition is once accepted that the integrity of the nation's institutions and the quality of its domestic life require a congenial international environment.[15]

It is no adequate response to these considerations to insist that in either of the above senses a policy of anticommunism is meaningless, if not counterproductive, in view of the diversity of forms "communism" now takes and the subordination by "communist" governments of ideological claims and affinities to national interests. True, communism means different things in different places, and sometimes different things even in the same place. But it does not follow that communism now means little more than that some people call themselves communists and, accordingly, that a policy of anticommunism pursues an unidentifiable mirage. Nor does it follow from the subordination of ideological claims and affinities to national interests that the expansion of communism no longer represents a threat to American interests. What follows from the plural-

---

[15] Rather than to charge American policy with a naive anticommunist obsession it is nearer the mark to say, as nearly all critics do, that it is obsessed with maintaining the status quo. Though this charge, too, is frequently overdrawn it is clearly the case that American foreign policy is the policy of a conservative power with a strong interest in order. In part, that interest reflects a fear that the way in which change may be expected to occur today will jeopardize the fabric of world peace. In part, however, that interest reflects a fear that change will be in a certain direction, that is, toward communism. The critics reply either that this last fear is unfounded or, to the extent it is valid, that it is the consequence of a self-fulfilling prophecy. But the issue is by no means so simple.

119

istic or polycentric character of communism today is that the expansion of communism can no longer be equated with the expansion of Soviet power (or with Chinese power). If this is undeniably a very significant development, it is still necessary to insist that little else can be deduced from the pluralism of the communist world. Pluralism means that communist regimes, where they are at all able to do so, will act independently and in terms of their own interests. It obviously does not mean that these interests will thereby cease to be inimical to American interests. Despite the reality of pluralism in the communist world, it still does not seem unreasonable to assume that a communist government in Central America is more likely to establish ties, including military ties, with the Soviet Union or China than with a noncommunist government. That it may do so for reasons of national interest and without thereby jeopardizing its independence, and that a major communist power may respond for reasons of national interest, are not decisive in determining whether the relationship represents a threat to American interests. Moreover, pluralism does not preclude an interdependence of action by communist states in response to irresolution shown toward a minor communist regime, and above all if the latter is allied to one or more major communist powers. An American defeat in Vietnam might lead to very different responses on the part of the Soviet Union, China, North Vietnam, and North Korea. That these responses are taken independently of one another does not mean they present no threat to American interests. Evidently, it does mean that there is less of a threat than if the states in question acted under central direction. But that may be all.

The absence of unity of action cannot be taken to imply the absence of interdependence of action. In either case, the deterrence of action may depend on substantially the same policy.[16]

It will not do, then, simply to indict American foreign policy for its blindness to the central political realities of the time and for its naive, though obsessive, anticommunism. What is primarily at issue is not these realities but their significance for American interests. What is primarily at issue is not an obsessive anticommunism that has no meaningful relation to American interests but the continued relevance of the American purpose to most of the world. Critics are right in pointing out that over the course of a generation American policy has been transformed from a policy that was Eurocentric, directed primarily against the expansion of Soviet power, and designed to restore a balance of power, to a policy that has become increasingly unlimited in geographic scope, motivated in part by fear that communism will prove to be the wave of the future in underdeveloped countries, and designed to preserve the status quo against revolutionary change (which is, in turn, nearly always equated

[16] A major point of many critics of Vietnam has been that the war cannot be won without the defeat of North Vietnam and that North Vietnam cannot be defeated without running a very grave risk of war with either the Soviet Union or China or both. Yet the same critics deride the view that a North Vietnamese victory can be seen as a victory for the Soviet Union or China, let alone as an extension of Soviet or Chinese power, and are skeptical that such victory will threaten American interests elsewhere as a result of the effect it may have on Soviet or Chinese policy. It is difficult to reconcile these propositions save perhaps through an insistence on the "unique" character of the Vietnamese conflict. That insistence, however, is less than compelling.

with communism). They are right in insisting that the pluralistic character of communism today—and, indeed, of the world—has not affected the conviction that world order forms an undifferentiated whole, that threats to this order are interconnected, and, consequently, that a challenge by a communist state or movement to one part of this order will very likely result, if unanswered, in challenges to other parts as well. Finally, there is no gainsaying their insistence that the inevitable outcome of this rationale is an imperial policy. Even so, the central issue remains whether this rationale and the policy which it supports respond to, and are necessitated by, the nature of American interests, not only as they are defined by the administration and its supporters but in large measure as they are defined by critics as well.

If the question thus posed appears little more than rhetorical to critics, it is principally because the realities of the contemporary world are not found to hold out a significant threat to the nation's vital interests. Why this is so will, of course, depend in part upon an analysis that varies from observer to observer. Thus there are differences in the estimates made of Soviet power today, in the evolution of Soviet policy, and particularly in the possibility —and desirability—of Soviet-American cooperation to insulate and pacify local disputes because of parallel interests in keeping their competition within safe limits, while blocking Chinese influence. Similarly, there are differences in the estimates made of Chinese power, if not actual then potential, as well as in the evolution of Chinese policy. Common to almost all analyses, however, is the conviction that a pluralistic world is a safer world.

Pluralism has given rise to a far more complicated world. It is still a safer world in that it must reduce considerably the threat held out to America's interests. Pluralism means that communist expansion, if and when it should occur, no longer carries the threat to American security that it once carried for such expansion no longer has the significance it once had. More important, however, pluralism means that the danger that communism will expand at all, whatever the altered significance of such expansion, has markedly and dramatically declined. For the triumph of pluralism is, in essence, the triumph of nationalism. Where a "communist" movement succeeds, then, as in Vietnam, it does so because it is able to identify more effectively with national aspirations than its competitors. Not only has this identification proven exceedingly rare among the underdeveloped countries, the indispensable condition for success, as Vietnam again shows, is the assertion and the reality of independence from outside control (not support, but control). And if this condition does not preclude the possibility of communist movements succeeding to power, it must limit the significance of such succession when and where it does occur.

The pluralist thesis does not conclude that there is no need for order, but that there is much less need for order, particularly in the southern hemisphere, than the ideologues of American foreign policy insist upon, and this because there is much less a threat to America's vital interests arising from changes—including violent changes—in the status quo than the official consensus is wont to pretend. It also concludes that what need for order there is can best be fulfilled—indeed, can only be

fulfilled—by other and, as it turns out, easier—
certainly less painful—means than those presently
employed. In sum, American policy both exagger-
ates the need for order and misconstrues the means
for maintaining it. In either case, the end result,
indiscriminate intervention, is the same.

Given the nature of American interests, however,
these conclusions are less than compelling. To be
sure, they would be compelling, or very nearly so, if
pluralism had the significance that critics commonly
read into it. But this is precisely what cannot be
assumed, for the evidence, such as it is, scarcely
proves the reading. Thus on the central issue of the
interdependence of the international system, hence
the interdependent character of American interests,
it is clear that this, and preceding, administrations
have consistently exaggerated the case, for reasons
already elaborated. But critics have also frequently
indulged in exaggeration by their reaction. Indeed,
some critics are quite willing to make the case for
interdependence "in reverse" when it suits their interests to do so. One of them writes: "The idea that
the frustration of a Communist bid for power in
South Vietnam will be some kind of decisive setback
for Communism in Southeast Asia or even in the
world is a political fairy tale. It fails to take into
account that no Communist bid for power which
forces the United States to pay such a high price
for 'victory' can be said to have been 'defeated.' If
the Communists of other impoverished, diminutive
Southeast Asian countries could be sure of making
us spend so much blood and treasure on frustrating
them, we might well be faced with an epidemic of
such wars. In this sense, the Vietnamese war, however it may end, has been more an encouragement

than a discouragement to other wars of 'national liberation.' . . ."[17] Why communists of other Southeast Asian countries should be tempted to repeat Vietnam, simply in order to make us spend so much blood and treasure on frustrating them, is left unexplained.

If it is absurd to equate interdependence with indivisibility, it is not absurd to insist that interests, though divisible, are interdependent. If it is exaggerated to insist that world order forms an undifferentiated whole, and that a challenge by a communist power to one part of this order is ipso facto a challenge to every part, it is not unreasonable to insist that world order is dependent upon the observance of certain restraints on the manner in which the status quo may be changed and that a successful breach of these restraints may encourage other, though perhaps dissimilar, breaches. Even if it is true that the war in Vietnam is unique and cannot be regarded as a test case for wars of national liberation, even if it is true that there is no such thing as a typical war of national liberation, it still does not follow that the outcome in Vietnam is without significance for what may—or may not—happen elsewhere. In international as in domestic society, the power of example, whether as a deterrent to disorder or as a challenge to order, does not depend upon the principle of identity.

A pluralistic world does not preclude an interdependent world. In part, this point is acknowledged by critics, though the attempt is made to restrict its significance largely to conventional interstate conflicts. The distinction is commonly drawn

[17] Theodore Draper, *Abuse of Power* (1967), p. 112.

between international and internal disorder, between international and domestic violence. In the case of violence that is clearly international there remains a need today, as in the past, for the ordering role played by great powers. But even here American policy has not escaped severe criticism for what is deemed the arrogant assumption that only this nation can bring order to the world. The practical results of that assumption are presumably apparent today in Asia, where the United States finds itself without the cooperation or support of any major power, though how it might have elicited this cooperation or support—particularly of the Soviet Union—is left unclear.[18] Be that as it may, this criticism does not affect the point that even conflicts between small states may prove detrimental to international stability and that as a great power America should try, in George Kennan's words, "to isolate, to moderate these conflicts, to settle them as quickly and easily as we can, not to worry too much about the issues, because there will be right and wrong on both sides, but to try to keep these local conflicts from doing great damage to world peace."[19]

[18] In this respect, as in a number of others, the general strictures of critics are unexceptionable and perhaps for that very reason not very illuminating. If the interests of policy can be obtained through joint, rather than unilateral action, then joint action is usually preferable, and particularly if unilateral action implies military intervention. The problem arises, of course, when a choice must be made between unilateral action or no action at all. And here we are confronted with yet another general stricture, equally unexceptionable: unilateral action, particularly military intervention, is justified only when a vital national interest is at stake. But when is a vital interest at stake?

[19] *Vietnam Hearings*, p. 386. Of course, no question arises where external aggression occurs against an area of vital interest to America.

The matter is otherwise in relation to internal or revolutionary wars. It is here, above all, that American policy is found to have erred in exaggerating the need for order while misconstruing the means for maintaining it. For pluralism means that, with few exceptions, in the confrontation of communism with nationalism, it is communism that must lose, particularly if we will but refrain from intervening. Again, it is George Kennan who sets the theme in declaring that "in most of these situations, in the smaller and developing countries, where there seems to be a threat of communism or of forces close to communism taking over, there are usually countervailing forces which, if we keep out, will make themselves felt. If we intervene we paralyze them."[20] The catalogue of American mistakes is by now familiar. Preoccupied with the need to maintain the status quo, and finding communism in every challenge to the status quo, we are driven to equate revolutionary violence with communism. Even where this equation is valid, the question remains in each case whether a communist regime would pose a threat to American interests. In the great majority of cases, however, the equation is not valid, at least not initially. Yet it may and already has increasingly become so through American insistence. By equating revolutionary violence with communism, by a policy of indiscriminate opposition to violent changes in the status quo, we assume the unenviable role of a counterrevolutionary power per se—a "glorified prison warden"[21] to the world—and either allow communist movements to seize the ban-

[20] *Ibid.*, p. 418.
[21] Steel, *Pax Americana*, p. 325.

ner of nationalism or force noncommunist revolutionaries into a communist stance.

The principal conclusion drawn from this critique is that intervention in revolutionary wars is either futile or unnecessary. Where a government is unable to suppress revolutionary forces primarily through its own efforts intervention is futile. Where a government is able to contain these forces primarily through its own efforts intervention is unnecessary. But if the immediate accent has been on the futility of intervention in the context of Vietnam, the larger view of critics has stressed the absence of a need to intervene in order to preserve essential American interests—of which, according to most critics, the general evolution of the underdeveloped states is one. If only we have the wisdom to refrain from making the fatal equation of revolution with communism, if we maintain at least a tolerant attitude toward reformist and even revolutionary movements which are noncommunist in character, and, finally, if we distinguish between communist movements and regimes in terms of the compatibility of their policies with American interests, the underlying forces at work in today's pluralist world afford little reason for anxiety. In a way, then, the principal conclusion critics reach manages to have the best of all possible worlds. Intervention in revolutionary conflicts may be futile in most cases and, in any event, beyond America's resources. Yet we need not despair, for what cannot be done generally need not have to be done in order to preserve American interests.

It is in the effects on the nation's purpose both at home and abroad that critics find perhaps the most serious indictment of American foreign policy. For that policy is considered to have betrayed the nation's purpose. The extent of that betrayal may be measured in the image America now projects to much of the world in contrast with the past. A generation ago America appeared as a self-confident nation whose foreign policy inspired confidence and trust. Today America appears anything but self-confident, and her foreign policy is no longer either wise or benevolent. Once a liberating force in the affairs of men, we are now the "world's self-appointed policeman," a "glorified prison warden" to the world. The "first revolutionary nation" has become the enemy of revolution. Nor are the effects of this counterrevolutionary position altered, or the judgment of others moderated, for the reason that American intervention has been inspired largely by fear of communism rather than by indifference to injustice and poverty.

This denial of the American purpose abroad cannot but have as a consequence the denial of that purpose at home as well. A preoccupation with the exercise of imperial power abroad has inevitably led to the neglect of needed internal reforms. Foreign affairs have thus become a surrogate for fulfillment at home. More generally, the alleged necessities of foreign policy, the awesome "responsibilities" of exercising imperial power, ultimately jeopardizes our domestic institutions and impairs the quality of our domestic life. "Our institutions," one observer declares, "were never designed for the role of an imperial power, even if empire is defined as an indirect hegemony like that of Athens; rather, our traditions of government were based on the assumption that the United States . . . would not need to enter the 'entangling alliances' of a major world power."[22] The quality of our domestic life is threatened if only because the foreign policies undertaken lack a rationale for intervention that is persuasive to the great majority. Nor can the recurring resort to violence abroad be without effect on the methods by which a nation solves its problems at home. Thus the leader of the opposition to Vietnam in the Senate has written: "If, as Mr. Rusk tells us, only the rain of bombs can bring Ho Chi Minh to reason, why should not the same principle apply at home? Why should not riots and snipers' bullets bring the white man to an awareness of the Negro's plight when peaceful programs for housing and jobs and training have been more rhetoric than reality?"[23]

These are the effects of American policy most commonly seen by critics. When taken together they form a recognizable theme and one that is deeply imbedded in the American tradition. Simply stated, that theme emphasizes the dangers inherent in too great a concentration on foreign affairs, a concentration that is considered to reverse the natural order of things. The corrective to these dangers, then, is apparent. The rehabilitation of American prestige abroad is dependent on the performance of America at home. The relevance of the American purpose in the world must come through the relevance and vitality of that purpose in America. Walter Lippmann articulates the view of a legion of critics in writing: "America can exert its greatest influence in the outer world by demonstrating at

[22] Roger D. Masters, *The Nation is Burdened* (1967), p. 118.

[23] Senator J. W. Fulbright, "The Great Society Is a Sick Society," *The New York Times* (August 20, 1967), p. 90.

home that the largest and most complex modern society can solve the problems of modernity. Then, what all the world is struggling with will be shown to be soluble. Example, and not intervention and firepower, has been the historic instrument of American influence on mankind, and never has it been more necessary and more urgent to realize this truth once more."[24] And Senator Fulbright urges: "The world has no need, in this age of nationalism and nuclear weapons, for a new imperial power, but there is a great need of moral leadership—by which I mean the leadership of decent example."[25]

There is no need to find in this position a reversion to isolationism, at least not in any historically recognizable sense of that term. It may, and indeed does, reflect a general view toward the significance of foreign policy. In this view, a society fulfills itself mainly by its domestic works; its greatness is measured primarily by its internal achievements. If there nevertheless remains a point at which foreign policy has primacy over domestic policy it is only because the security and independence of the state are regarded as the indispensable means to the protection and promotion of individual and societal values. To this extent, foreign policy is a "necessity," on the whole a rather burdensome and unwelcome intrusion, the ultimate justification of which must be its contribution to domestic happiness and welfare. Even so, there is no necessary relationship between this general view of the significance of foreign policy and a policy of isolationism, if only for the reason that what is considered indispensable to security in the broader sense may still lead to a policy that is

[24] "Notes from a Holiday," *International Herald Tribune* (May 11, 1968), p. 4.
[25] "The Great Society Is a Sick Society," p. 90.

anything but isolationist. The necessities of foreign policy may be decried, but the integrity of the nation's institutions and the quality of its domestic life may still be judged to require an international environment that implies a very extensive definition of vital interests. Moreover, it is clear that a renewed emphasis on the primacy of domestic policy need not be seen to reflect a skepticism toward, let alone an abandonment of, the American purpose and its continued relevance for the world. The conviction that America may yet regenerate mankind, though now once again by the power of her example, remains an article of faith for many critics. Thus Senator Fulbright can decry the arrogance of recent American foreign policy, yet conclude that: "at this moment in history at which the human race has become capable of destroying itself, it is not merely desirable but essential that the competitive instinct of nations be brought under control. . . . [America,] as the most powerful nation, is the only nation equipped to lead the world in an effort to change the nature of its politics."[26] What separates a Senator Fulbright from those he has so persistently and effectively criticized is not so much a disagreement over the American purpose in the world as it is a disagreement over the manner in which that purpose is to be achieved.[27]

[26] *The Arrogance of Power* (1966), p. 256.

[27] Compare the quoted statement in the text above with these words of President Johnson, taken from his first major address following the initiation of aerial bombardment against North Vietnam: "Our generation has a dream. It is a very old dream. But we have the power and now we have the opportunity to make it come true. For centuries, nations have struggled with each other. But we dream of a world where disputes are settled by law and reason. And we will try to make it so."

132

Still the question remains: has America betrayed its purpose, if only by the manner in which it has sought to achieve it? In domestic affairs the question has become meaningful, or, at least, urgent, only in the context of the Vietnamese conflict. For it is only since 1965 that a persuasive case can be made for the debilitating effects of foreign on domestic policy. It is true that since the late forties some have insisted that the demands of the cold war have represented a continuing threat to the viability of American institutions and have generally resulted in the marked impoverishment of domestic life. But this theme has largely rested upon a comparison of what had been done to improve the quality of domestic life with what might have been done if foreign policy had not been paramount. That juxtaposition, however, proves very little, since we have no assurance that what might have been done in the absence of the cold war would in fact have been done. If anything, experience suggests that the contrary proposition is equally, if not more, plausible. What is beyond conjecture is that the nature of the hegemonial competition in which the nation was engaged did provide much of the impetus for the domestic change that was undertaken.

Vietnam, on the other hand, clearly has had a debilitating impact internally. It has been deeply divisive, more so than any issue of the past generation, and has debased the standards of public discourse and behavior. Moreover, if the cold war often acted as a stimulus to domestic change that otherwise would not have been undertaken, Vietnam has reversed this pattern and has either retarded or frustrated needed social reform both by creating a fierce budgetary competition between foreign and domestic expenditures and by siphoning off mental and spiritual resources. It is no adequate response to point out that the nation can now afford its Vietnams and its great national tasks. It does not wish to pay for both and apparently cannot be induced to do so. Nor is it an adequate response to argue that even with the war government efforts in the fields of health, education, aid to the poor, and aid to urban areas have tripled in less than a decade. What matters is men's definition, which may undergo sudden change, of what constitutes a tolerably just society. What matters is that after many years of relative neglect expectations have been aroused and demands have been made which can be frustrated only at considerable risk.

At the same time, if Vietnam has shown that the internal face of reason of state can be malignant, the extent of that malignancy ought not to be exaggerated. An imperial policy might well lead in time to the derangement of our political institutions, but Vietnam has not had this effect. On the contrary, its principal effect has been to cause the Senate to assert a degree of independence in the area of foreign policy that is perhaps greater than at any time since the pre-World-War-II period. And if the war has contributed to the debasement of standards of public discourse and behavior, it has not eroded civil liberties. If anything, the war has provided a notable occasion for the exercise of these liberties. Moreover, the recent debasement of public standards is not simply, and perhaps not even primarily, the result of the war. The penchant to attribute to the war almost all that is unsettling and alarming in American public life is understandable.

It is not for this reason correct. That Vietnam coincided with both a racial and generational crisis scarcely proves that the war precipitated, let alone caused, either crisis. That Vietnam has exacerbated both in some measure is clear, though in what measure it is next to impossible to say. Yet in view of the long standing massive indifference shown by an affluent white majority toward the plight of a black minority, to emphasize a tie between violence in Vietnam and violence in America's ghettos appears too much like a form of special pleading. At the very least, it is to push at a door that was already wide open. Nor are there persuasive reasons for believing, despite the gravity of the racial crisis, that the door might once be closed if Vietnam can only be terminated and future Vietnams avoided. Too much has been made of the argument that the denial of the American purpose at home is the consequence of a preoccupation with the exercise of imperial power abroad. Foreign affairs may have become in part a surrogate for fulfillment at home, but it is also true that failure at home has other, and deeper, roots.

These considerations apart, the view that America can exert its greatest influence in the world today through the power of its example at home evidently rests on two assumptions: that influence is primarily a matter of example and that the American example must continue to be relevant to the world. Even if we were to accept the latter assumption, however, it does not follow that the former assumption is valid. Let us suppose that we were to set the best of examples at home. Let us suppose that we demonstrate, in Walter Lippmann's words, "that the largest and most complex modern society can solve the problems of modernity." This is without doubt a very ambitious task. But even if it were to be seriously and effectively undertaken there is no persuasive, or even plausible, reason for believing that it would somehow resolve the problem of maintaining a world order in which American interests would be preserved. Why should the example that we set at home affect Chinese aspirations in Asia? Why should the example that we set at home affect the prospects of nuclear proliferation? How would a benign example on our part resolve the conflict between the Arab states and Israel? There is something touching in the belief for which history, including our own, provides little basis, that we can do by example what we cannot do by precept. It reflects, if nothing else, the ironic nature of our present position in the world. When contrasted with our earlier expectations that position, and the policy to which it has given rise, must indeed appear to have little relation to the traditional purpose of America. For that purpose was never seen to imply that we should play the role of policeman to the world. It did imply that the day might come when we would have to free the world, but surely not to police it. One polices the world because men and nations are recalcitrant, because they often have deeply conflicting aspirations, and because they are influenced more by precept than by example—even the best of examples.

Nor would it matter a great deal if men were influenced more by example than by precept. If example has been the historic instrument of American influence on mankind, the relevance of that example today is no longer clear apart from the industrialized states of the West. For most of the world, for the underdeveloped states that comprise the southern hemisphere, we are not going to serve as an example, however model our behavior at home, because our example is irrelevant to their experience and to the problems they must solve. No one can say with assurance what example these states will ultimately emulate. It is not difficult, however, to make a persuasive case for "the probability that the political force most likely to succeed in carrying through the gigantic historical transformation of development is some form of extreme national collectivism or communism."[28] The "Metternichs" of American foreign policy are not, as critics would have us believe, the mindless prisoners of pernicious myths in fearing this outcome. They may be deluded in thinking the outcome can be averted, let alone controlled, by America. They may be deluded in believing that the integrity of American institutions and the quality of American life would otherwise be substantially impaired. But they are not deluded in taking the prospect of this outcome seriously. This is not to say that critics are wrong in insisting upon a far greater concentration on domestic problems. It is only to say that this concentration must be justified in its own terms, which is, after all, surely justification enough.

[28] Heilbroner, "Counterrevolutionary America," p. 31.

IV. CONCLUSION

In a period of a few weeks in the spring of 1968 what had been the great verities of postwar American foreign policy suddenly seemed to become the great uncertainties. Whereas for years it had been generally assumed that the broad lines of American policy were fixed, suddenly it seemed that nothing was fixed. What had long appeared, to the satisfaction of most and the despair of few, as the massive continuity of policy suddenly seemed little more than a fragile edifice which, once it began to crumble, gave the lie to the "stability of mood" that had been found increasingly to characterize the public's response to foreign policy. Instead of the "end of either/or,"[1] so confidently predicted in the preceding year by one close observer of and high participant in American policy, there appeared the prospect of a change in mood and policy as great as preceding changes the nation had experienced in this century. The prevailing temper of uncertainty found an almost plaintive expression in the assertion—or plea— of one articulate spokesman of an imperial America that although "American foreign policy, after this trauma, will never again be the same," we still "can't resign as policeman of the world."[2] Yet to many observers the question posed earlier in this essay—

[1] McGeorge Bundy, "The End of Either/Or," *Foreign Affairs* (January 1967).
[2] Irving Kristol, "We Can't Resign as 'Policeman of the World,'" *The New York Times Magazine* (May 12, 1968), p. 25.

nation or empire?—already seemed to have lost much of its relevance.

In large part, the rash of prophecies of far-reaching change in American foreign policy has been prompted by the experience in Vietnam. Yet the meaning of this experience for American foreign policy remains unclear. It is of course quite clear that the public wants no more Vietnams and cannot be expected to support them. It is equally clear that future administrations will ignore this public disposition only at their peril. But this does not say a great deal about the future course of American foreign policy, given the distinctive characteristics that have marked the conflict in Vietnam. To the extent that the reaction to Vietnam has been a response to those features which have set this war apart from other wars the nation has waged, it may afford little indication of what the public can or cannot be induced to support, or, at least, to tolerate. Moreover, it is well to recall that despite the distinctive characteristics of the war—the uncertainty over its immediate origins, the dispute over the identity of the aggressor, the elusiveness of the objectives of the war, the seeming indifference of those on whose behalf the war was being fought—opposition did not achieve significant proportions until the demands imposed by the war reached a certain level. Even then, it was the inability of the administration to make a persuasive case for believing military victory was possible, let alone imminent, without a still greater commitment of men and material that proved to be the breaking point. On the basis of these considerations, we cannot know a great deal about the limits public opinion may impose on the future use of American power. We cannot know, for example, whether the reaction to Vietnam fore-shadows a similar reaction to interventions in areas of more traditional interest, particularly if the cost of intervention can be kept relatively modest. That the public cannot be expected to support Vietnams does not mean that it can be expected to tolerate little more than Dominican Republics. If the cost of intervention remains a critical determinant of public tolerance or opposition, the significance of Vietnam for future constraints imposed by public opinion must be read with caution.

To be sure, the opposition to Vietnam must be attributed to other factors as well. Although the cost of vindicating the interests for which intervention was presumably undertaken in Vietnam ultimately proved too high, and in the end this consideration was decisive, it is still true that Vietnam was opposed throughout on other and broader grounds. Indeed, it was these other and broader grounds that in large measure made the cost of the war seem too high. Vietnam could not be effectively represented either as a vindication of the principles of freedom and self-determination or as a measure indispensable to American security. Yet it is difficult to estimate the extent to which these considerations will limit the use of American power in the future. Vietnam and the ensuing debate have shown that there is a broad disparity of view over both the conditions and even the very meaning of American security as well as over other interests the vindication of which would justify the use of American military power. But there are no indications that this disparity of view will soon be resolved. Thus the failure to employ effectively the security argument in the case of Vietnam need not be taken to mean that the same argument would fail elsewhere, quite apart from the merits with which it might be made. The insistence with which many opponents of the war continue to declare that the United States can tolerate no more Castros in the Caribbean or Central America is, in this respect, instructive.

In part, speculation on significant and even radical changes in American foreign policy is based on changes in the international and domestic environment that have been long in the making and that Vietnam has dramatically revealed. These changes, it is argued, are so profound and far-reaching as to reverse what has heretofore appeared as something close to a law of history. Whereas in the past power has almost invariably created its own interests, the latter expanding in rough proportion to the former, we are now presumably on the threshold of an era, if, indeed, we have not already entered it, in which this apparently "natural" process will no longer hold true. It will no longer hold true because the external restraints on the use of power—above all, military power—are not only greater than they have ever been in the past but so great as to challenge the traditional meaning of statecraft. At the same time, and largely as a result of these restraints, the stakes of foreign policy seem more elusive and problematic than ever for those states whose physical security can be jeopardized only by a nuclear conflict. Hence the question arises: Is the game any longer worth the candle? Why should the great nuclear powers contend over the allegiance of the underdeveloped states when the instruments of power they may bring to bear are increasingly circumscribed, when the competition is costly, and when the stakes of the competition are elusive? And if the third world disappears as an object of contention, what remains for the great powers to contend over?

Moreover, to the restraints imposed by the international environment must be added the restraints imposed by the domestic environment. With nations as with individuals, the real revolution of rising expectations is not among the poor but among the affluent. Whether in America or in Europe, or even in the Soviet Union, the consumer's desire for more continues to increase disproportionately to an ever expanding economy, while the margin of resources with which governments must conduct foreign policy appears to decrease in proportion to the economy. Nor are the domestic constraints simply a function of the consumer's desire for more. They are also a function of the largely unforeseen problems generated by advanced and affluent societies. We have come to discover that the rich too have their problems and that, even if they are not insoluble, they may be very difficult problems. Finally, in America's case, the domestic restraints on foreign policy may be distinguished not only by virtue of a racial crisis that has no parallel elsewhere in the advanced societies but by the emergence of a generation that does not know, and apparently cannot believe in, the problem of insecurity—at least, in the conventional sense. The depths of this skepticism are revealed not only by the reaction of the younger generation to Vietnam but even more significantly by the approval increasingly shown toward revisionist interpretations of the origins of the cold war. Contrary to common expectation, this almost radical skepticism shown toward the security claims of the state may prove in the end to have a greater impact on foreign policy than any other factor.

142

These tendencies in the international and domestic environment may indeed eventuate in far-reaching changes in American foreign policy. At present, however, they remain tendencies whose consequences are largely indeterminate. Although the restraints on the use of power appear greater today than in the past, they have not changed the traditional meaning of statecraft. It is not necessary to explain Vietnam in terms of these novel restraints and may even be misleading to do so. Nor does it follow that once the stakes of foreign policy have become elusive that states will thereby give up the game. Physical and economic security apart, the interests over which men and nations have contended in the past have always had an elusive quality. Yet their quality of elusiveness has seldom persuaded men to abandon them. Whether it will do so in the future, whether affluent societies that no longer have a serious security problem will become progressively disinterested in the traditional stakes of foreign policy, must remain a matter of conjecture.

Rather than speculate over what American foreign policy can be in the aftermath of Vietnam we conclude this essay by asking what it should be. We cannot, of course, usefully ask what American policy should be without also asking what it can be, that is, without making some assumptions about the scope of possible change. The foregoing considerations suggest, however, that we cannot know the scope of possible change. Indeed, these considerations indicate that in the aftermath of Vietnam American foreign policy can take any one of a number of directions; they point to a broad range of possibilities none of which is clearly foreclosed by the necessities

of either the domestic or the international environment. Thus we cannot appreciate the significance of
Vietnam for future domestic restraints on foreign
policy. These restraints may become apparent in the
course of four or five years. They are not apparent
today. Much will depend upon the manner and terms
by which the war is brought to an end. If the undertaking in Vietnam can no longer issue in success, it
still holds out a broad choice of failures. Both in its
purely domestic repercussions as well as in its effects
on public willingness to support future interventions, the nature of the choice is evidently of considerable importance.

What is true of the internal restraints on foreign
policy is almost equally true of the external restraints. The latter are no longer apparent largely
because the security requirements of the nation are
no longer apparent, which is, as we have emphasized
throughout in these pages, what the debate has
above all been about.

The general issue of security is that great, though
unresolved, issue of the debate. It will not do, then,
simply to intone about the external circumstances
which limit possible foreign policy choices, for it
is the very meaning today of these circumstances in
relation to the nation's security and well-being that
is at issue.

The external constraints on policy are apparent,
or very nearly so, if it is assumed that the nation's
security remains dependent upon the purposes and
objectives of the Truman Doctrine and of the successive policies of containment. This assumption
forms the core of the administration's rationale for
the American commitment in Vietnam. What is at
stake in Vietnam, the familiar argument runs, is

nothing less than the principles on which the peace of the world is to be organized and maintained. Is that peace, and the order it implies, to be one of consent or one of coercion, one which safeguards the right of self-determination or one which destroys this right, one which provides an environment favorable to the growth of free institutions or one which encourages the spread of arbitrary and irresponsible power? The fundamental issue raised by Vietnam, then, is the issue of world order, an issue that cannot be separated from American security.

The equation of world order and American security is not only central to the administration's defense of Vietnam, it must also be central to any projection of what American foreign policy will be in the aftermath of Vietnam. In the absence of substantial, and even fundamental, changes in the international environment, changes which would facilitate the task of maintaining international order, the imperatives of American policy must have much the same significance in the future that they have had in the recent past. So, too, in the absence of a more favorable international structure of power, America has no choice but to maintain intact its present commitments, even if it does not add to them. The need for order cannot be expected to diminish with a termination of the war. If anything, a settlement in Vietnam that falls short of America's initial objectives must be expected to increase this need, by virtue of the encouragement it will give to the forces of disorder and the insecurity it will create among those dependent upon American protection. Not the least of the consequences of this insecurity might be a sharpened interest in obtaining nuclear weapons on the part of nations which do not presently possess these weapons but are capable of making them. The likelihood of this consequence alone is considered persuasive not only of the continuing need for order and of America's responsibility to meet this need, but of the persisting inseparability of world order and American security.

The equation of world order and American security does not, as such, mark a departure from an earlier period. It is true that a conventional security purpose was paramount in the early policy of containment. It is equally true that as initially applied to Europe containment was more or less synonymous with a balance-of-power policy. But if a narrower and more traditional conception of security was primary in early containment policy, it never excluded a broader purpose, which derived from a concept of world order set forth by the Truman Doctrine. The Truman Doctrine, in turn, emphasized the need of employing American power and leadership to create and maintain a stable world order, an order which would enable peoples to work out their own destinies in their own way and, by enabling them to do so, thereby insure American security. In part, then, the contrast many critics have drawn between the relatively precise purposes of early containment policy and the vague purposes of policy today is instead a contrast between the circumstances attending the application of policy then and now. For the circumstances of an earlier period limited the application of containment principally to Europe and made that application, whatever its larger purpose, roughly identical with a balance-of-power policy.

The change in emphasis from containment to world order thus reflects a change in circumstances rather than, or as much as, a change in purpose. It reflects, as already noted, both the success of the initial policy of containment and the expansion concomitant with that success of American interests and the diversity of possible threats to them. At the same time, the change in circumstances that has attended, and in part resulted from, this success and expansion lays bare the principal difficulty of the rationale given for American policy today, a difficulty so clearly illuminated by Vietnam. For it was a narrower and more traditional conception of security that led to the transformation of American policy in the late nineteen-forties. It was the fear that domination of western Europe by the Soviet Union might shift the world balance of power decisively against the United States that above all prompted the historic departure in American foreign policy. The broader purpose of the Truman Doctrine clearly facilitated that departure. Even so, it did not form the indispensable mainspring of change. To put the matter differently, if the broader purpose of the Truman Doctrine was also equated from the start with the nation's security, it was still the narrower conception of security—security interpreted in terms of a balance of power centered in Europe—that provided the essential basis for early containment policy not only in Europe but in Asia as well. It is the change in the structure of American security, and not simply the change in the scope of American interests and commitments, that must account for the shift in emphasis from containment to world order, just as it is the change in the structure of American security that must account for the principal difficulty encountered by the administration in defending its commitment in Vietnam. To say this is neither to dismiss the equation of American security and world order nor to deny the applicability of that equation to Vietnam. It is to insist that many, if not most, of America's present interests and commitments are primarily the result of a conception of security that can no longer satisfactorily account for these same interests and commitments.

These considerations point to the conclusion that it is not so much the vagueness of world order as a purpose of American policy that is at issue but the desirability and, even more, the necessity of this purpose. As we have sought to show elsewhere,[3] there is nothing unusually vague about this purpose so long as its operational significance is understood. That it is commonly articulated in terms of general principles which may have little tangible and immediate relation to the realities of power is understandable. That these general principles may lead to difficulties and even to contradictions if the attempt is made to apply them consistently and without regard to power realities is equally understandable. Given the nature of international society—the small number of members, the normal lack of consensus among them, the absence of effective mechanisms for peaceful change, the prevalence of self-help— such order as this society may enjoy at any time must have a quite specific meaning and one that finds its primary expression in a given structure or distribution of power. However abstract the nature of the order described by American statesmen and however general the principles on which this order is presumably based, it, too, has a quite specific meaning in practice. It, too finds its primary expression in a structure of power the principal and, indeed, the

[3] Cf. pp. 53–66.

only substantive threat to which is held to emanate from communist powers. The principles on which this order is based are not applied with a fine consistency and impartiality. If the resort to aggression by others is never condoned, it still is considered to hold out a serious threat to world order only when undertaken by communist powers. If the suppression of freedom is never approved, it still is considered to hold out a serious threat to world order only when undertaken by organized communism. The operational meaning of the American objective of world order is largely synonymous with opposition to the expansion of communism. World order is, in practice, containment writ large. Whatever else may be said of this order, the charge of vagueness seems misplaced.

It is another matter to question the desirability and necessity of world order as a dominant purpose of American policy. The question of necessity, at least, turns on the issue of security. That issue may be simplified if a distinction is drawn between the narrower and broader meaning of security, that is, between the physical and more than physical dimension of security. In its narrower meaning the case for equating American security and world order evidently depends upon showing that the failure to maintain world order would measurably increase the danger of involving this nation in a nuclear war, for it is this contingency alone that can today threaten America's physical security. It will not do, however, to argue that if an attack upon America's vital interests would involve this nation in a nuclear war, the preservation of these interests is therefore vital to America's physical security. Although it is probably true that America would risk nuclear war to prevent western Europe and Japan from falling under the control of a hostile power, it is also true that the reason for taking this risk would not be security in the narrower sense. For the loss of these areas would not as such threaten the nation's physical security, though their loss might well threaten the nation's security in a broader sense.[4] Thus what would probably involve this nation in a nuclear war is by no means synonymous with what would threaten America's physical security. There is nothing novel in this apparent paradox of nations—and particularly great nations—risking their physical existence over interests which would not jeopardize their physical existence if lost. What is novel is that nuclear weapons illuminate the issue more clearly than ever before.

There is one interest which, if lost, could possibly, if not very plausibly, threaten America's physical security. That interest is in preventing the further spread of nuclear weapons. In its simple, though essential, form the view that emphasizes the interest in preventing nuclear proliferation is tied to world order and, in turn, to America's physical security in the following manner. The world is terribly in need of order today, an order that presupposes American

---

[4] If security is equated with physical security, and, in turn, considered in its traditional sense as a function of a balance of power, America has faced a security problem only during two relatively brief periods. It did so during the two decades between the founding of the Republic and the Louisiana Purchase. It did so again during the two decades between the early nineteen-thirties and the early nineteen-fifties. In the history of nations, this benign experience must be considered unique. It must also in part account for the expansive concept of security entertained by this nation.

leadership, because without order and the consequent security it brings nations feeling themselves insecure will be impelled to obtain nuclear weapons. Once that happens, the world will become progressively less stable, if only because with more nations possessing nuclear weapons the prospects must increase that some among them will attempt to use these weapons in order to change the status quo. The danger of nuclear war will thereby increase as a result of nuclear proliferation and with the increase of that danger will go the increase of the danger that America, along with the other nuclear powers, will ultimately become involved. Thus it has been argued, in the context of the controversy over Vietnam, that a failure to maintain order in Southeast Asia, that is, to vindicate the American commitment in Vietnam, might well lead to a decision on the part of India and Japan to acquire nuclear weapons.

At best, the necessity allegedly imposed by the interest in preventing nuclear proliferation rests on assumptions we have no way of validating. One such assumption is that the prime candidates for nuclear weapons will prove less prudent and responsible than the present nuclear powers. We have no persuasive reason, however, for accepting this assumption, just as we have no persuasive reason for assuming that the compulsion—or temptation—to use nuclear weapons to change the status quo will be greater for future nuclear powers than for present possessors of these weapons. Nor is it apparent why any and all nuclear confrontations or conflicts would, indeed must, involve this nation. They would involve us, of course, if it is assumed that America retains unchanged its present interests and commitments. But this assumption establishes a vital American security interest in nonproliferation only by begging the principal question at issue. If this assumption is not made, the threat to American security arising from nuclear proliferation must largely depend upon the argument that a nuclear peace is indivisible. The argument obviously cannot be based upon historical evidence. The fervor with which it has been put forth does not alter its speculative character. A nuclear peace might prove just as divisible as any other peace.

What is not speculative are the consequences of accepting this view of the American interest in preventing nuclear proliferation. It affords, if accepted, a perfect rationale for freezing indefinitely the international power structure and present international hierarchy. It also affords a perfect rationale for the indefinite exercise of imperial power. We cannot reasonably expect that in the foreseeable future the present nuclear powers will either destroy their weapons or surrender them to some international authority. Yet in the absence of such action we also cannot reasonably expect the international power structure to undergo significant change, since the possession of nuclear weapons is the indispensable prerequisite of great power status and, ultimately, of independence as well. In the absence of such action, then, how would we ever be able to divest ourselves of our great responsibilities for maintaining international order? Surely not by sharing these responsibilities with those who already possess nuclear weapons, for two of the other four possessors are presumably the main threat to order—indeed, the only substantive threat to order.

Thus, in the absence of a Japan and India armed with nuclear weapons and able to provide not only for their own security against China but eventually perhaps even to contain China in East and Southeast Asia, how are we to divest ourselves of our great responsibilities in Asia? To argue that nuclear proliferation in Asia would be one of the effects of failure in Vietnam, thereby presumably demonstrating the importance of not failing in Vietnam, is persuasive only to those who wish to see no basic change in America's Asian policy. Far from being an unwanted effect, proliferation is perhaps the one prospect for creating an indigenous Asian balance of power, a balance that would clearly permit us to divest ourselves of our great responsibilities in that region.

If the insistence upon finding in nuclear proliferation a threat not only to world order but to America's physical security is less than persuasive, it does afford an insight into the fundamental ambivalence of American policy. The persistent official refrain that "we are not the world's policeman," while impossible to take literally, is a least indicative of an aspiration whose sincerity need not be impugned. America is perhaps history's example par excellence of the state that reluctantly, and apologetically, acquired imperial power. But if we did not want the position we acquired, having acquired it we also do not want to let it go. This reluctance is not refuted by constant reiteration of a desire to lighten America's burden by sharing power and responsibility with others. It is not enough to aspire to a diffusion of power and a devolution of responsibility if the means necessary to this end are denied. It is not enough generally to aspire to a diffusion of power while, at the same time, resisting a diffusion of the ultimate form of power. Admittedly, this resistance is in part the result of a genuine fear—unfounded or not—about the spread of nuclear weapons, a fear that cannot be separated from the reluctance to return to a more traditional system of interstate politics (a reluctance in turn manifested in the vague and apolitical prescription of regionalism). In part, however, it is simply the reluctance imperial powers have always shown to let go of what they have.

It is clear that the plausibility, let alone the persuasiveness, of equating world order and American security must rest upon a broader and even a transcendent meaning of security in which necessity inescapably merges with desirability. It is not the nation's physical existence that is at issue but the integrity of its institutions and, more generally, the quality of its domestic life. Do these interests, the protection of which may risk the nation's physical existence, require the maintenance of what we have defined as a congenial world order? Do they require the maintenance of our present interests and commitments abroad, interests and commitments that are or have become roughly synonymous with our conception of world order? Are they compatible with a greater degree of disorder and instability, a marked reduction of American influence, and an improved prospect for communist movements in the developing world?

These questions must be pressed in any serious criticism of American foreign policy. For the consequences they suggest are the probable consequences of a substantive change in policy. It is not enough to call for the abandonment of "globalism" and "interventionism" without acknowledging the effects of this prescription if followed. In fact the majority of the articulate and influential critics are not disposed to accept some or any of these consequences, in part because they believe that the most important change required is really one of style or outlook rather than of policy itself, in part because their principal disagreement is over the methods rather than the interests of policy, and in part because they entertain a relatively optimistic assessment of the nature of the threat posed to American interests. Thus it is characteristic of much criticism that a radical critique of America's diplomatic style is attended by remarkable forebearance in urging specific changes in policy. Yet however important the matter of style, the critical issue of policy remains one of interest and commitment. Moreover, the crux of that issue today does not concern interests and commitments we do not have but those we do have. It does not advance matters greatly to insist that we take on no further commitments, particularly when there is very little likelihood of this occurring. The vital question is what we should do with our present commitments, both formal and informal. If the answer is nothing, then a change in style may still leave unchanged the substance of policy. And if it is argued that however unwise it may have been to have entered into many of our present commitments, to abandon them now involves unacceptable risks, how does this position differ in its policy implications from the position taken by the administration and its supporters?

To be sure, there are many critics who insist that the issue is not one of letting go of what we have, of abandoning our major interests, but one of how best to vindicate those interests. The containment of

China, the general evolution of the underdeveloped states, above all the avoidance of nuclear war—these and other interests are not in real dispute. It is instead the means of policy that have given rise to serious differences, and this dispute over means reflects in turn widely varying estimates of the threat posed to commonly acknowledged interests. But the difficulty of the argument attacking the means of policy is precisely that it rests upon a questionable analysis of the threat held out to American interests. It finds in the pluralism of today's world a refutation not only of the interventionist's conviction of the great need for order but of the means by which this order has been maintained. What evidence we have of the effects of pluralism, however, scarcely proves the critics' optimistic reading.

The difficult truth to accept is that the nature of American interests, not only as they are defined by the administration and its supporters but in large measure as they are defined by the critics as well, must broadly account for the methods of American policy. The latter cannot be seriously altered without altering the former. If American policy is interventionist today, it is because of the nature of American interests and, of course, the nature of the world in which these interests are to be realized. It is not enough, then, to attack the "pernicious myths" of American policy, which have presumably led to interventionism, while leaving aside the essential interests of policy. What, after all, are these myths? Is it really a myth, for example, to equate revolutionary violence with communism in the underdeveloped states? If it is, then the "myth" appears to have as much an empirical basis as the alleged "reality." The issue is not whether this equation has made of us a counter-revolutionary power, for it has evidently done just that,[5] but whether the equation is, on the whole, correct. Where are the revolutions, where are the pervasive restructuring of societies required by development, that are noncommunist? Critics are fond of posing what is to them no more than a rhetorical question: How many of the states of the third world have gone communist? The answer, however, may well be another rhetorical question: How many of these states have had a meaningful revolution?

The abandonment of an interventionist policy, particularly in Asia, will mean a greater degree of international instability. (For it will mean, in substance, the abandonment of the policy of containing Asian communism, whether Chinese, North Korean, or North Vietnamese.) It will lead to a substantial reduction of American influence in the world, a reduction that cannot be compensated for by the power of the example we set at home. (We may be better liked as a result, though even this is uncertain, but we will still have less influence.) And it will lead to an improved prospect for the emergence to power of communist movements in the developing world. Must these consequences be prevented? Would their occurrence jeopardize the integrity of the nation's institutions and the quality

[5] There is a very great difference, however, between contending that we have been counter-revolutionary and contending that, in so being, we have thereby helped to create communists where there were none. Critics very often equate these contentions, but that equation is, at best, tenuous. It assumes that the forces eventually impelling underdeveloped societies to extreme collectivist solutions are largely of America's creation. This assumption, in its way, attributes almost as much influence to America as the assumption that the outcome of the great historical transformation of development can be controlled by America.

157

of its domestic life? Can America regenerate itself only by seeking to regenerate the world as well? Only the dogmatic will find categorical answers to these questions. Still, they must be answered and the answer given here is a negative one.

It is a negative answer largely for the same reasons that Vietnam has proven seriously debilitating in its domestic effects.[6] These effects cannot be avoided in the future simply by taking greater care to obtain public consent to critical foreign policy decisions than has been the case with Vietnam. No doubt it is true that a significant part of the opposition to Vietnam has come from the public's sense of exclusion from participation and involvement in the decisions that lead to the war and to its subsequent escalation. There seems little basis, however, for the view that this sense of exclusion provided the principal source of opposition to the war, that the war was opposed mainly because "a majority of people believed the war undemocratic—waged in violation of the tradition of consent which is fundamental to the effective conduct of foreign policy in a free society."[7] This view not only overestimates the public's expectations of applying the processes of democracy to foreign policy, it also ignores that consent may always be given retroactively. Besides, why was it that the necessary degree of popular consent to the vital decisions of the war was either not obtained or not kept? Surely not because this consent was undesired and unsought. Surely not because the reasons for making the vital decisions of the war were left

---

[6] Cf. pp. 128–37.

[7] Bill D. Moyers, "One Thing We Learned," *Foreign Affairs* (July 1966), p. 661.

unexplained and undefended. No war in American history has been explained and defended more by an administration than Vietnam. If these efforts ultimately failed the failure was not one of communications but of what was communicated. Despite an intense and unremitting effort at persuasion, in the end the sacrifices entailed by the war could not be justified. They could not be effectively justified because security, however broadly conceived, could not be effectively equated with purpose, whether in Vietnam or in Asia generally. And they could not be justified because, in the context of Vietnam, the conviction grew that purpose itself was being betrayed.

If Vietnam has a deeper lesson to teach it is that the American purpose cannot be sought after in today's world save through methods which must threaten the denial of this purpose. For the pursuit of world order, as we have conceived of world order, must frequently require intervention in the internal life of states. A refusal to admit this consequence follows from an insistence upon finding the requirements of order only in the external relations of states. On this view, the causes of and reasons for intervention are external. Of course, the requirements of international order are finally external. But it is precisely the mark of a revolutionary period that the roots of external disorder are, in large measure, internal. This being so, the attempt to maintain a certain kind of order in the relations between states almost inevitably must mean the attempt to bring about a certain kind of order within states. An imperial policy can thus scarcely avoid the repetition of Vietnams.

America's historic purpose of universalizing the

American experiment can only be betrayed by such a policy. For that purpose, as critics quite rightly point out, has mainly rested, and necessarily so, upon the power of example. The irony—and to some the tragedy—of America's position today is that at the height of her power her purpose has become increasingly irrelevant to most of the world. The course of wisdom is to accept this outcome and, at the same time, to abandon the conviction that America can only regenerate herself by regenerating the world.